D1602191

1

Table of Contents

Introduction

The NES Elementary Education Exam is designed to prepare elementary teachers for the classroom by ensuring that they have a strong knowledge base in the content areas that they will be expected to teach. These content areas are divided into two separate subtests. Subtest I tests the areas of Reading and English Language Arts and Social Studies. Subtest II tests the areas of Mathematics, Science, and The Arts, Health, and Fitness.

The Test at a Glance

Test	Subtest I (102)	Subtest II (103)
Format	75 multiple choice questions	75 multiple choice questions
Time	1.5 hours	1.5 hours
Delivery Method	Computer	Computer
Areas Tested	<ul><li>Reading and English Language Arts (62%)</li><li>Social Studies (38%)</li></ul>	<ul><li>Mathematics (50%)</li><li>Science (38%)</li><li>The Arts, Health, and Fitness (12%)</li></ul>

Each of these subtests has multiple topics that will be explored in the rest of this guide.

Reading and English Language Arts

Reading and language arts are foundational for student success. Students develop skills in reading, writing, and speaking that demonstrate comprehension of written and spoken texts, a command of the mechanics of the English language, and critical thinking skills.

Test Structure

The Reading and English Language Arts section is the largest section of Subtest I. It consists of 47 multiple choice questions (62% of the subtest). Within Reading and English Language Arts, there are five major subcategories with which you must be familiar:

A. Foundations of Language Development and Emergent Literacy

B. The Development of Phonics, Word Analysis, Spelling, and Fluency

C. Reading Comprehension and Vocabulary Skills

D. Types of Texts

E. Written and Oral Communication

Each subcategory is divided into topics, which state the skills you must be able to demonstrate on the exam.

The foundations of literacy are those early stages during which students gain the basic literacy skills that will be the building blocks for their future reading and writing. It is important to support these foundations because gaining these skills early in life sets students up to be more successful throughout their future.

Topics Addressed:

1. Language Development

2. Listening Skills

3. Phonological and Phonemic Awareness

4. Concept of Print, the Alphabetic Principle, and Letter-Sound Correspondence

Foundations of Language Development and Emergent Literacy

There is important language development that occurs even before a child can read or write words. This is known as emergent literacy. These skills are developed from birth and include listening, speaking, memory, recognizing pattern and rhyme, print awareness, critical thinking, and the development of the fine motor skills necessary for writing.

The Role of Oral Language Development in Emergent Literacy

Oral language plays an important role in emergent literacy. Linguistic awareness—the ability to understand sound structures within language—is an essential oral language skill. In order to one day be able to read and write, children need to be able to hear the ways in which language is separated into parts. As they listen to oral language, they begin to recognize similar sounds, rhymes, and, eventually, syllables. Being able to not only recognize but also produce these word parts and patterns orally is an important early step in emergent literacy. Early exposure to frequent language with a wide vocabulary is important to children's linguistic development.

Factors Affecting Language Development

There are many factors that affect the rate and manner in which children's language abilities develop. Some of these factors include:

- Developmental and medical issues
- Health of the home environment
- Socioeconomic status
- Socialization and exposure to a variety of texts, people, and experiences that provide new vocabulary

Building on Students' Current Language Skills

Because student backgrounds and skill levels are so diverse, it is essential for teachers to meet students where they are and build on their current language skills. They should identify current areas of strength to build on, while identifying and correcting areas of weakness. Instruction needs to be differentiated for the wide array of literacy skills that will be part of the classroom population.

Listening skills are essential to literacy. Because so much early literacy is developed through oral communication, listening skills are an integral part of literacy development. Students must be able to listen carefully to a speaker, glean information aurally, and produce an appropriate response. It is therefore essential to promote listening skills in the classroom.

Listening is more than just hearing words. To listen, understand, and make meaning from spoken words requires active listening. There are several ways to be an effective listener:

- Focusing on the speaker
- Making eye contact
- Following directions
- Responding to questions appropriately
- Paying attention to non-verbal communication
- Developing auditory memory

Phonological awareness is a broad skill that involves the understanding that language is made up of sound units (i.e. words, syllables, onsets, rhymes, etc.) and the ability to manipulate those units.

Phonemic awareness is a more specific skill that involves recognizing and manipulating phonemes, the smallest sound units within words.

Fundamental Phonological Awareness Skills:

- **Rhyming**- having an ending sound that corresponds with another (e.g. *cat, hat*)
- **Alliteration**- having the same beginning sound
- **Segmenting**- the ability to break a word up into its individual component sounds
- **Blending**- combining sounds to form words

Promoting Phonological Awareness Skills

Helping students understand phonemes and develop the ability to manipulate them is essential to their early literacy development. Some of the exercises with phonemes that are helpful for literacy development are:

- Using music, nursery rhymes, or other memorable jingles to introduce children to sounds, rhyming, and the rhythms and patterns of speech
- Phoneme isolation- recognizing separate phonemes in words
- Phoneme segmentation- separating a word into all of its phonemes
- Phoneme identification- finding common phonemes among different words
- Phoneme blending- giving a sequence of phonemes that create a word
- Phoneme addition- making a new word by adding a phoneme to an existing word
- Phoneme deletion- removing a phoneme from a word to make a new word
- Phoneme substitution- replacing a phoneme with another to form a new word

Three foundational emergent literacy skills are the concept of print, the alphabetic
principle, and letter-sound correspondence.

Concept of Print

Understanding the concept of print is the awareness that written letters have sounds
and that they form words. Children should learn the structure of a book and have
repeated exposure to text.

Alphabetic Principle

The alphabetic principle is the understanding that words are made up of letters that
have different sounds. This is developed through exposure to text and print.

Letter-Sound Correspondence

Letter-sound correspondence is the knowledge of the sounds that are associated
with each letter of the alphabet.

The Development of Phonics, Word Analysis, Spelling, and Fluency

The section covers literacy development as it moves from the emergent stage into more formal structures.

Topics Addressed:

1. The Role of Phonics and Sight Words
2. Phonics Patterns and Word Analysis Strategies
3. Decoding and Encoding
4. Fluency
5. Promoting Literacy Skills for Diverse Learners

Phonics is the understanding the sounds and printed letters are connected. Groups of sounds (with their associated letters) are organized into sequences to form words. Phonics provides a way for students to decode and encode words based on their component sounds.

Sight words are those short, familiar words which students come to recognize visually ("on sight") without having to decode the sounds.

Both phonics and sight words play an important role in literacy development. Sight words help children to get a jump-start on reading and to be able to tackle many small words that they will encounter frequently without having to spend the time and mental energy breaking them apart in order to decipher them. Phonics, meanwhile, gives students the skills they will need to tackle unfamiliar words and progress further in their literacy development with increasingly sophisticated words.

Phonics Patterns

Phonics follow certain predictable patterns. Within the system of phonics, there are letters or combinations of letters that make certain sounds. Words that contain these same sounds are said to contain the same phonics pattern. Teaching phonics patterns helps children with decoding by familiarizing them with common letter(s)-sound pairings. Some common phonics pattern types are:

- Long vowel sounds (the "a" in "ate," "rake," "shade")
- Short vowel sounds (the "i" in "hit," "tip," "crib")
- The long ("moon") and short ("good") "oo" sound
- Digraphs- two consonants together that make a new sound (the "ph" in "photo")
- Consonant blends- combination consonant sounds (the "ft" in "gift")
- Hard and soft c and g sounds

Morphology

Morphology is the study of morphemes, which are the smallest units of sound that have meaning. These can include roots, prefixes, and suffixes. Students with a knowledge of morphemes and their meanings are better equipped to decode and decipher the meaning of new words. Instruction in morphemes gives students an important tool for the structural analysis of words.

Syllabication

A **syllable** is a unit of sound that contains one vowel sound. Onset and rime are subdivisions of syllables. **Onset** is the initial consonant sound of a syllable and **rime** is vowel sound plus the remainder of the syllable. For example, in the word "brick," "br" is the onset and "ick" is the rime.

Syllabication is the ability to correctly divide words into syllables. For developing readers and writers, syllabication helps to break words up into chunks that are easier to handle.

Decoding

Decoding is the ability to apply the knowledge of letter-sound relationships in order to pronounce written words. Decoding requires several skills of its own. To successfully decode a word, a learner must be able to know the letters in the word and their appropriate sounds, remember each of these sounds in sequence, and put the sounds together to create a word.

Encoding

Encoding is the ability to convert oral language into text. In order to encode, children must recognize the phonemes within words, know the letters that correspond with those sounds, and be able to put those into writing.

Stages of Writing Development

As children grow and develop, so do their writing skills. From their earliest scrawling eventually develops fully written compositions. Teachers should be familiar with how this process unfolds.

Stage	Description
Drawing	Expresses ideas through pictures; uses drawing as a form of communication
Scribbles	Uses scribbles as a form of writing; intends the scribbles to have meaning like writing
Letter-like Forms	Shapes start to look like letters but are not actual letters
Pre-communicative / Random letters	Writes actual letters but in patterns or strings that make no sense, uses letters without appropriate letter-sound correspondence
Invented spelling	Begins to form words but with own spelling; sometimes phonetic spelling; sometimes a single letter may stand for syllables or whole words; transitional spelling-improves over time
Conventional spelling	Spells correctly and resembles adult writing

Fluency is the ability to read text smoothly, without paying much conscious attention to the mechanics of reading. As learners' literacy skills develop, their fluency increases over time. Whereas beginning readers must decode and sound out many words, fluent readers give no thought to this and are able to read with speed and accuracy. Once readers become more fluent and no longer have to spending their time and mental energy decoding words, they can focus more on comprehension.

Fluency is measured by two main components—rate and accuracy.

- **Rate**- the speed at which reading occurs
- **Accuracy**- a measure of the percentage of oral reading that is correct

A diverse student population requires adaptation on the part of the teacher to ensure that the needs of each student are being met. Students come to the classroom with a wide range of backgrounds, prior knowledge, and skills that will result in a classroom whose readers are on many different levels of proficiency.

Some ways to promote literacy skills for a diverse group of learners are:

- Utilizing pre- and post-assessments
- Leveled reading materials
- Scaffolding
- Cooperative learning
- Differentiated assignments and assessments
- Modeling
- Guided practice
- Assessments that vary in form (standardized, portfolio, project-based, anecdotal, performance tasks, etc.)
- Goals based on growths models

Promoting Literacy Development in Second-Language Learners

One particular subgroup in the classroom that may need extra support in language development are second-language learners. Depending on the individual student, second-language learners may have varying degrees of literacy both in their native language and in English.

Some basic principles to promote successful literacy for these students are:

- Place value on the literacy skills they already possess, including those in their native language.
- Utilize and enrich first-language knowledge.
- Ensure that English as Second Language (ESL) instruction is at a developmentally appropriate level but is also age-appropriate and challenging enough to maintain interest.
- Provide explicit vocabulary instruction.
- Provide ample exposure to rich language input.
- Maintain open communication, provide positive feedback, and encourage peer relationships.

Speaking, listening, and viewing play an important role in language acquisition for second-language learners. Mastery of a language requires the ability to read, write, and speak in the language, and listening and viewing can help to promote the development of those other skills.

For second-language learners, especially in the early stages, frequent opportunities for listening and viewing are essential. Listening enables learners to hear the language aloud and begin to pick up its pronunciation and rhythms. Tone and context are also often easier to detect in spoken language than in written language, which can help the listener to understand more of what is being said. Listening is also essential for learning conversational English, which can be different than conventional written English.

Viewing is also important for second-language learners. Visual aids are tremendously helpful for students trying to learn new vocabulary. It helps them to remember words and creates a link between a written or spoken word and something concrete.

Speaking is often one of the most difficult tasks in learning a second language. Often, learners are able to understand far more language than they are able to correctly produce. Providing ample opportunities for speaking practice in a non-threatening environment is important for their language development.

This section covers the development of comprehension and vocabulary skills, as well as strategies for promoting those skills amongst diverse readers.

Topics Addressed:

1. Factors Affecting Reading Comprehension

2. Literal, Inferential, and Evaluative Comprehension Skills

3. Promoting Reading Comprehension

4. Vocabulary Development

Comprehension is the ability to understand read content, process it, and think about it critically. Comprehension takes reading beyond fluency— which just requires words to be pronounced correctly and fluidly—and into a process in which the words take on deeper meaning.

Factors Affecting Reading Comprehension

There are many factors that affect a child's ability to comprehend written text. These include:

- Background knowledge
- Fluency
- Vocabulary
- Comprehension skills
- Use of comprehension strategies
- Motivation
- Structures and features of the text

The three major types of reading comprehension are literal, inferential, and evaluative comprehension.

Literal comprehension is understanding of the meaning of the words in a passage. This can include tasks like:

- Stating the main idea of a passage
- Identifying the topic sentence of a passage
- Identifying supporting details

Inferential comprehension is using information explicitly stated in the passage to determine information that is not stated.

- Making predictions
- Identifying implicit relationships such as compare/contrast; cause and effect
- Inferring implicit meanings

Evaluative comprehension involves analysis and/or making judgments about the information presented in the text. This can include tasks like:

- Drawings conclusions based on evidence in the text
- Determining the author's purpose
- Distinguishing fact from opinion
- Making connections between the text and other sources or situations

There are many strategies students can employ to increase their reading comprehension. Here are several common ones:

- Annotating texts
- Drawing on prior knowledge to make inferences, make connections, and draw conclusions (also called inferential reading)
- Metacognition—awareness of one's own knowledge; self-monitoring to assess progress, identify difficulties, and employ strategic problem-solving
- Multi-pass strategies such as SQ3R (Survey, Question, Read, Recite, Review)
- Pre- and post-reading exercises such as K-W-L (Know, Want to Know, Learned)
- Summarizing
- Using graphic organizers

Vocabulary acquisition is an important part of literacy development. As readers mature, they should gain a more extensive vocabulary. There are several tools that can help students to interpret new vocabulary:

- **Affixes**- common beginnings (prefixes) and endings (suffixes) that add meaning to a base word. Understanding the meaning of an affix can help students make sense of the word.

Common Prefixes	Common Suffixes
A-	-er
Bi-	-est
Tri-	-ing
Un-	-ly
Pre-	-fy
Non-	-it
Dis-	-is
Anti-	-tion

- **Root words**- the most basic form of a word that conveys meaning. Many words in the English language have root words from other languages, such as Greek and Latin. There are hundreds of root words in the English language but a few examples are listed in the chart below.

Root Word	Meaning	Example
Aqua	Water	Aquatic
Demo	People	Democracy
Geo	Earth	Geography
Mal	Bad	Malice
Mono	One	Monologue
Poly	Many	Polytheism
Omni	All	Omniscient
Script	Write	Manuscript

- **Context clues**- information in the text surrounding a new word that help provide meaning

Types of Texts

This section covers the various types of texts that elementary students may encounter.

Topics Addressed:

1. Components of Literature
2. Genres of Children's Literature
3. Informational, Persuasive, and Functional Texts
4. Graphic Sources

There are many types of literature written for children. They fall under two general categories—fiction and non-fiction. **Fiction** is material that not an accurate account of real people and events but rather is imagined by the author. **Non-fiction** is material that is presented as being factual and accurate.

Major Types of Literature

The major forms of fiction and non-fiction literature include, but are not limited to, those listed in the chart that follows:

Fiction	Non-Fiction
<ul><li>Drama (play)- a piece meant for performance, where the story is presented through dialogue</li><li>Novel- a book-length narrative that presents its characters and plot with a degree of realism</li><li>Poetry- literature written in verse</li><li>Short story- a brief work of narrative prose</li></ul>	<ul><li>Autobiography- an account of the author's own life</li><li>Biography- an account of another person's life</li><li>Diary (or journal)- a dated, personal record of events over a period of time</li><li>Essay- a short piece intended to express an author's point of view on a topic</li><li>Letter- written correspondence from one person to another</li><li>Textbook-a book used to study a particular subject</li></ul>

Components of Narrative Story-Telling

Narratives share several major common elements:

- **Setting**- when and where the story takes place

- **Theme**- the underlying idea of a story

- **Plot**- the events in the story; there are five parts to a plot:

  1. Introduction- the characters, setting, and necessary background information are introduced

  2. Rising action- the story becomes more complex and the conflict is introduced

     The types of conflict are *man vs. man, man vs. self, man vs. nature, man vs. society,* and *man vs. fate.*

  3. Climax- the height of the conflict and turning point of the story

  4. Falling action- the conflict begins to resolve itself

  5. Resolution- the conflict is resolved and the story concludes

- **Characters**- the people (or sometimes animals or objects) who participate in a story

  The two main types of characters are the **protagonist** (the main character or hero) and the **antagonist** (the character that works against the protagonist).

- **Point of View**- the perspective from which the narration takes place; who is telling the story

  o Main Types of Narrators:

    1. First person- ones of the characters tells the story from his or her own perspective; uses "I"

    2. Third person- the story is told by an outside voice who is not one of the characters

    3. Omniscient- a third person narrator who knows everything about all of the characters, including their inner thoughts and feelings.

    4. Limited omniscient- a third person narrator who only knows the inner thoughts and feelings of one specific character

Literary Terms and Figurative Language

Figurative language is writing that goes beyond the literal meaning of the words and uses comparison to convey meaning.

Term	Definition	Example
Alliteration	Repetition of a beginning consonant sound; considered figurative language because it can help create mood and imagery	The lonesome lady left one last, long, look for her love.
Hyperbole	Exaggeration for emphasis	I'm so hungry I could eat a whole elephant!
Idiom	A phrase that has come to have a different meaning through usage than the meanings of its individual words	Something easy is said to be "a piece of cake."
Imagery	Descriptive writing that appeals to the senses	The rich aroma of coffee drifted through the air, bringing warmth on a bitter January morning.
Metaphor	A comparison between two things that does not use "like" or "as"	He is a chicken.
Onomatopoeia	Words that convey sounds	Buzz, crackle, pop, bang
Oxymoron	Combining two words with opposite meanings	Jumbo shrimp
Personification	Giving human characteristics to nonhuman things	The leaves danced as the wind whistled through the trees.
Simile	A comparison between two things that uses "like" or "as"	Cool as a cucumber

The Basic Elements of Poetry

Poetry is a form of creative literature written in verse. Poetry can take many forms, several of which are listed in the chart below:

Form	Definition
Acrostic	A poem in which the first letter of each line forms a word when read from top to bottom
Ballad	A poem narrating a story in stanzas, often quatrains
Blank Verse	Poetry that is metered but not rhymed
Cinquain	A five line poem with specified syllabic emphasis, depending on the type of cinquain
Concrete	A poem written into a familiar shape relating to the poem's meaning
Elegy	A poem about someone's death
Epic	A long poem about the adventures of a hero
Free Verse	Poetry that is neither rhymed nor metered
Haiku	A Japanese form of poetry that contains three lines of 5, 7, and 5 syllables, in that order
Limerick	A humorous five-line poem with a rhyme scheme of AABBA
Lyric	A poem expressing personal emotions
Ode	A lyric poem addressed to a particular subject, which often contains lofty imagery
Sonnet	A fourteen-line poem

Poetry also has its own unique vocabulary of terms, including techniques that poets employ in creating their works.

Term	Definition	Example		
Alliteration	Repetition of a beginning consonant sound	"Peter Piper picked a peck of pickled peppers."		
Assonance	Repetition of vowel sounds	"As I was going to St. Ives, I met a man with seven wives."		
Consonance	Repetition of consonant sounds anywhere in the words	"Hickory, Dickory, Dock, The mouse ran up the clock. The clock struck one, The mouse ran down. Hickory, Dickory, Dock."		
Foot	One unit of meter	**Type of Foot**	**Definition**	
		Iambic	Unstressed syllable followed by a stressed syllable	
		Trochaic	Stressed syllable followed by an unstressed syllable	
		Spondaic	Two stressed syllables in a row	
		Pyrrhic	Two unstressed syllables in a row	
		Anapestic	Two unstressed syllables followed by a stressed syllable	
		Dactylic	Stressed syllable followed by two unstressed syllables	
Meter	The rhythm of a poem, dependent on the number of syllables and how they are accented			
Mood	A poem's feeling or atmosphere			

Term	Definition	Example	
Repetition	Using a word or phrase more than once for rhythm or emphasis	"Show men dutiful? <u>Why, so didst thou</u>: seem they grave and learned? <u>Why, so didst thou</u>: come they of noble family? <u>Why, so didst thou</u>: seem they religious? <u>Why, so didst thou</u>."	
Rhyme	The repetition of ending word sounds; can be *internal rhyme* (within a line) or *end rhyme* (the words at the end of the lines rhyme with each other)	Internal rhyme: "Jack <u>Sprat</u> could eat no <u>fat</u>." End rhyme: "Little Miss <u>Muffet</u> Sat on a <u>tuffet</u>"	
Rhythm	The pattern of sounds with a poem		

Term	Definition	*Name*	*# of Lines*
Stanza	Groups of lines of poetry; named for how many lines they contain	Couplet	2
		Triplet	3
		Quatrain	4
		Quintain	5
		Sestet	6
		Septet	7
		Octane	8

Term	Definition	*Name*	*# of Feet*
Verse	A line of metered poetry; named for the number of feet per line	Monometer	1
		Dimeter	2
		Trimeter	3
		Tertameter	4
		Pentameter	5
		Hexameter	6
		Heptameter	7
		Octometer	8

Basic Elements of Drama

Drama is a literary form in which the story is presented through dialogue and is meant to be performed for an audience. Common forms of drama intended for children include:

- Plays
- Skits
- Puppetry
- Story theater

Drama is covered in more detail in the Arts, Health, and Fitness section.

Literature for children is written in many different genres. The chart below shows some of the major ones.

Genre	Description
Allegory	Story in which the characters and events represent ideas or concepts
Drama (play)	A piece meant for performance, where the story is presented through dialogue
Fable	A short story with a moral lesson
Fantasy	Stories involving make-believe that often occur in imaginative realms with creatures or powers that do not exist in real life
Folktale	A story passed down through oral traditions
Historical fiction	Story that takes place in the past and is realistic for that time period
Myth	A story created to explain natural or social phenomena
Non-fiction	Factual information
Parable	A short story used to teach a moral lesson
Poetry	Stories or ideas expressed through verse
Picture book	Illustrated stories where the text and pictures are interdependent
Realistic fiction	Fiction that takes place in the contemporary "real world" with characters and situations that are believable
Science fiction	Story created by extending scientific ideas to imaginary, though logical, conclusions; often set in the future
Tall tale	An exaggerated story, usually about a real person

Non-fiction writing can be classified as informational, persuasive, or functional.

Informational Texts

Informational texts are meant to teach the reader facts about a subject.

Examples:

- Biography
- Textbook

Persuasive Texts

Persuasive texts are meant to convince the audience of a point of view.

Examples:

- Editorial
- Persuasive essay

Functional Texts

Functional texts provide instructions for the reader.

Examples:

- How-to guide
- Instruction manual

Graphic sources include such visual aids as charts, graphs, illustrations, photographs, editorial cartoons, diagrams, tables, and multimedia sources. They are used to reinforce and enhance textual information by representing the information in a different or more detail manner. Graphic sources help readers to visualize information.

Viewing various media requires its own skill set. This includes:

- Interpreting images- finding meaning in visual cues
- Evaluating media techniques- identifying the methods used to create the media and present its message and assess their effectiveness
- Understanding the message- deriving the purpose of the media and the overall idea it is trying to convey

Written and Oral Communication

This section covers the process and conventions of writing, including grammar and syntax. It also covers the elements of effective speaking.

Topics Addressed:

1. The Writing Process

2. The Structure and Elements of Communication

3. Conventions of Standard American English

4. The Elements of Effective Writing and Speaking

Structures and Organization of Writing

Writing can take on many forms and be organized in many ways. Structures of writing are devices that help the writing to accomplish its purpose. Some examples of writing structures are:

- **Description**- a writing mode for creating a mental picture of someone or something
- **Definition**- provides a statement of the exact meaning of something
- **Argument**- presents a case in favor of a particular point of view or opinion
- **Examples**- provide evidence to clarify an idea, add details, or to give support to an argument

The organization of a piece can help the writing to fulfill its purpose by conveying meaning in the most effective manner.

Term	Definition
Descriptive	Provides a detailed description of someone or something
Comparison/Contrast	Examines the similarities and differences between two or more things
Cause and Effect	Presents causal relationships between a particular event or idea and those that follow it
Persuasive	Aims to convince the reader of a point of view; will include arguments and supporting evidence
Problem-Solution	Presents a problem, suggest and explains a possible solution, and discusses the potential effects of the solution
Sequential	Presents events in chronological order or presents a set of ordered steps

The Five Stages of the Writing Process

As students learn to write, it is important for them to learn to write according to a clear process in order to ensure that their writing is given thought and quality. Throughout the writing process, peer editing can be a valuable tool to help students evaluate and revise their work.

1. **Prewriting-** brainstorm ideas for writing

2. **Rough Draft-** write down all of the ideas in an organized way

3. **Revise-** reread the rough draft and make changes to how the information is presented and organized; make sure tone, purpose, and audience are clear; add or delete content as needed

4. **Edit-** make changes to spelling, grammar, and other mechanics

5. **Publish-** create the final copy

Evaluating and Incorporating Resources

There are many resources available to teachers in reading and language arts. In addition to traditional print materials, multimedia resources can be used to enhance literacy learning. Teachers should become familiar with the resources available in their schools and communities and integrate them into classroom learning. Additional, students should be familiarized with resource materials that they can use for research and to enhance their writing and presentations.

Sources of information fall under two major categories—primary and secondary sources.

Primary sources are original sources that give a first-hand account of an event by someone who participated in it or observed it at the time that it was happening. Some examples of primary sources are diaries/journals, letters, interviews, and surveys.

Secondary sources are created later by people who did not experience events first-hand. They draw on primary sources as their own source material and present their collected research to the reader. Some examples are research articles, books, and encyclopedias.

When evaluating sources, teachers and students should check for reliability, bias, accuracy, and up-to-date information.

There are two main types of communication—intrapersonal and interpersonal. Elementary-level students should be given instruction and support as they develop their skills in both of these areas.

Intrapersonal Communication

Intrapersonal communication takes place within one single person, and includes that person's own thoughts and feelings. Some of the important elements of intrapersonal communication are:

- Self-concept: how a person views him or herself
- Attitude: feelings about a subject or situation
- Beliefs: what a person thinks to be true or false, good or bad, etc.
- Values: deeply rooted ideals, closely tied to beliefs
- Perception: how a person sees the world
- Goals and expectations: what a person wants or expects to happen
- Internal discourse: thought processes or imagined conversations
- Speaking to oneself aloud
- Writing to oneself (i.e. journaling)

Interpersonal Communication

Interpersonal communication is that which occurs between people. Interpersonal communication can include:

- Conversation
- Group discussion
- Written communication (email, letter, text, etc.)
- Public speaking
- Mass communication

The main components of written language are grammar, usage, and syntax. **Grammar** is the set of guidelines which govern the proper use of language. **Usage** refers to the proper use of words. **Syntax** is the manner in which words are arranged into sentences.

Parts of Speech

The basic types of words which make up the English language are known as parts of speech.

Part of Speech	Definition	Examples
Noun	Person, place, thing, or idea	boy, ball, Utah, democracy
Pronoun	Word that can take the place of a noun	he, it, something
Verb	Word that reflects an action or state of being	run, be
Adverb	A word that modifies a verb	quickly, very
Adjective	Descriptive word	happy, cold
Preposition	A word that indicates direction or position, or connects two ideas	on, off, above, to, of, from, at
Article	A word that comes before a noun that indicates whether the noun is specific or non-specific	a, an, the, this
Conjunction	A words that joins two words or phrases	for, and, nor, but, or, yet, so

Nouns

There are several different ways to classify nouns.

- Common vs. Proper

    o **Common noun**- general thing or idea; does not require capitalization. Examples: girl, country, religion

    o **Proper noun**- refers to a specific person, place, thing, or idea and DOES require capitalization. Examples: Alicia, Canada, Buddhism

- Singular vs. Plural

    o **Singular**- refers to only one thing. Examples: apple, goose

    o **Plural**- refers to more than one thing. Examples: apples, geese

- Subject vs. Object

    o The **subject** of a sentence is who or what the sentence is about. The subject performs the main verb of the sentence.

    o The **object** of a sentence is not the main subject of the sentence and has the verb *performed on it.*

    Example: *"Lisa enjoys listening to music."* In this sentence, "Lisa" is the subject and "music" is the object.

- Concrete vs. Abstract

    o **Concrete noun**- physical object. Examples: rock, building

    o **Abstract noun**- non-physical things, like ideas. Examples: creativity, sadness

Pronouns

Pronouns take the place of more specific nouns. The noun that a pronoun stands for is called the **antecedent.** Example: *"Daniel works as a financial planner. He has worked at the same company for ten years."*

In this example, "he" is the pronoun and "Daniel" is the antecedent.

Just like nouns, pronouns can be classified as subjects or objects.

- Subject pronouns: he, she, I, we, they

- Object pronouns: him, her, me, us, them

Pronouns can also show possession.

- Examples: her, his, my, mine, ours, their

Verbs

There are three major types of verbs—action, linking, and helping.

- **Action verbs** show an action performed by the subject of a sentence.

    o Example: She <u>ran</u> to the store.

- **Linking verbs** connect the subject of the sentence to the additional information about the subject.

    o Example: The cat <u>was</u> black.

- **Helping verbs** are paired with another verb and are often used to indicate tense.

    o Example: School <u>will</u> be open tomorrow.

Verbs also indicate the time period in which the action is taking place. This is called **tense**. There are three major tenses—present, past, and future.

- **Present tense**- the action is occurring now

    Example: Anna lives in New York City.

- **Past tense**- the action occurred in the past

    Example: Anna lived in New York City.

- **Future tense**- the action will occur in the future

    Example: Anna will live in New York City.

Syntax

Syntax is the manner in which words are arranged into sentences. There are rules that govern proper syntax. A sentence must contain both a subject and a predicate.

- **Subject-** the part of the sentence that is *performing* the action; the noun that the sentence is about

  Example: <u>Many trees and bushes</u> grow in the forest.

- **Predicate-** gives information about the subject

  Example: Many trees and bushes <u>grow in the forest.</u>

A sentence *may* also contain one or more objects. As stated above, an object is a noun that receives the action of the verb. Objects can be direct or indirect.

- **Direct object-** directly receives the action of the predicate; answer the questions "whom?" or "what?"

- **Indirect object-** indirectly receives the action of the predicate; answer the questions "to whom/what?" "from whom/what?"

- Example:

  "I gave a treat to the dog."

  Subject- "I"

  Direct object- "treat"

  Indirect object- "dog"

Words are grouped together in several basic forms.

- **Phrases** are the most basic grouping of words. The words are related but may lack a subject (e.g. "went swimming) and/or a predicate (e.g. "my mother").

- **Clauses** are groups of words that contain both a subject and a verb. There are two types of clauses:

  - **Independent clause-** expresses a complete thought and could stand alone as a complete sentence

  - **Dependent clause-** does not express a complete thought and therefore could not stand alone as a complete sentence

- Example:

   "Because he got a flat tire, Tim was late to work."

   "Tim was late to work" is an independent clause because it could stand alone as a complete sentence.

   "Because he got a flat tire" is a dependent clause because it could not stand alone as a complete sentence.

- **Sentences** are groups of words that contain both a subject and a predicate and express a complete thought.

Types of Sentences

A **sentence** is a grammatical structure that includes both a subject and a predicate and expresses a complete thought.

There are four main types of sentences:

1. **Declarative-** makes a statement and ends with a period.

   Example: My dog's name is Bruno.

2. **Imperative-** gives a command and usually ends with a period.

   Example: Give me that pencil.

3. **Interrogative-** asks a question and ends with a question mark.

   Example: Will you eat dinner with us tonight?

4. **Exclamatory-** shows strong feeling and ends with an exclamation point.

   Example: I'm so happy to see you!

Sentence Structure

There are four main types of sentence structures:

1. **Simple sentences** contain one independent clause.

   Example: I went to the store.

2. **Compound sentences** contain two or more independent clauses, joined by a conjunction or punctuation mark.

   Example: I went to the store and I bought eggs.

3. **Complex sentences** contain one independent clause and at least one dependent clause.

   Example: On my way home from work, I went to the store.

4. **Compound-complex sentences** contain at least two independent clauses and at least one dependent clause.

   Example: On my way home from work, I went to the store and I bought eggs, then I stopped for gas.

Elements of Writing

All writing contains three main traits—tone, purpose, and audience. Keeping these in mind while writing and being intentional about the message you want to present is the best way to write effectively.

- **Tone-** the feeling or attitude that a piece of writing conveys
  Examples: humorous, sad, serious, uplifting
  Ensure that the tone is clear and appropriate for what you are trying to accomplish with the piece of writing.
- **Purpose-** why the author wrote the piece; what is the goal of this piece of writing?
  Examples: to persuade, to entertain, to inform
  Keep this purpose in mind throughout to maintain focus of the goal of the writing. This will help to inform tone and language choices.
- **Audience-** who the piece is intended for; who is supposed to be reading this?
  Examples: children, adults, women, sports fans
  Ensure that the reading level and writing style are appropriate for that audience.

Elements of Speaking

When speaking, the speaker must take into consideration several aspects of the speaking process. Just like writing, speaking involves purpose, audience, and tone; however, since speaking is a live process rather than something that will be read later, and since the speaker will usually be visible to the audience, other special considerations must come into play. A speaker should make these considerations:

- **Purpose-** Why are you speaking? What do you hope to accomplish?
- **Tone-** What feeling should this have? Funny? Serious?
- **Audience-** Who are you speaking to? What are they like? What are their wants and needs?
- **Occasion-** When and where is this taking place? Is what you are saying appropriate in this setting?
- **Speaker-** How should you present yourself? What preparations should you make? Non-verbal communication is very important. Ensure that your body presents confidence and focus.

Social Studies

Social Studies introduces students to topics in history, geography, and social science in an effort to equip them to become informed and contributing members of a democratic society.

Test Structure

The Social Studies section is the second section of Subtest I. It consists of 28 multiple choice questions (32% of the subtest). Within Social Studies, there are three major subcategories with which you must be familiar:

A. Government and Economics

B. United States and World History

C. Geography and Social Studies Inquiry

Each subcategory is divided into topics, which state the skills you must be able to demonstrate on the exam.

Government and Economics

This section covers the major forms of government systems, with special focus on the structure of the United States government. It also addresses foundational concepts of economics and economics systems and how those effect the world.

Topics Addressed:

1. The Structures, Functions, and Purposes of Government

2. The Levels and Branches of Power in the U.S. Government

3. Principles of Democratic Citizenship

4. The Organization of World Politics

5. Economic Concepts and Systems

6. The Influence of Competition, Markets, and Prices

Governments are created to maintain order in a society and for the protection of individuals' lives, liberties, and properties. Governments establish laws in order to protect these things and to prevent conflicts among people.

Functions of Government

Regardless of the type of government, there are several functions that a government is expected to carry out. The type of government will influence how to and what extent these are enacted.

The basic functions of government are:

- Establishing laws
- Public safety
- Maintaining order
- Providing public services
- Defense
- Economic activity
- Education

Structures of Government

In order to carry out these functions, governments consist of some form and combination of the following basic structures:

- Legislature- makes the laws
- Court system- provides justice and settles disputes
- Executive-enforces the laws
- Bureaucracy- carries out the day-to-day functions of the government

The United States is considered a democratic republic. The operations of its government are outlined in the **United States Constitution**.

The government of the United States is a **federal system**, which means that power is divided between the national and state governments. Powers allocated to the national government (e.g. the military, warfare, interstate commerce, coining money) are called **delegated powers**. Powers that belong to the states (e.g. professional licensing, intrastate commerce, establishing schools) are called **reserved powers**. Powers that are shared by both the national and state governments (e.g. taxation, making laws, having courts) are called **concurrent powers**. Within each state, there are also local governments that make day-to-day decisions affecting their communities.

At the national level, power is divided between three branches of government. This **separation of powers** ensures that no one person or group has all the power. The branches are the executive, legislative, and judicial branches. Each branch has its own responsibilities, which include **checks and balances** on the other branches.

	Executive Branch	Legislative Branch	Judicial Branch
Who?	President, Vice-President	Congress (House of Representatives and Senate)	Supreme Court
How Chosen	Elected for 4-year terms	House: elected for 2-year terms Senate: elected for 6-year terms	Appointed by the President and approved by Congress; serve for life
Main Duty	Enforce the laws	Make the laws	Interpret the laws
Checks on Other Branches	• Appoints Supreme Court nominees • Can veto laws	• Must approve Supreme Court nominees • Can override presidential veto • can impeach president of Supreme Court justices	• Can declare laws or presidential actions unconstitutional

The Constitution was intended to be flexible, allowing it to change as necessary with the times. This is why it includes a process for adding **amendments**, or changes, to the document. Currently, there are twenty-seven amendments. The first ten amendments are collectively known as the **Bill of Rights** and they outline citizens' basic rights and freedoms.

The Bill of Rights	
1st Amendment	Freedoms of speech, religion, press, assembly, and petition
2nd Amendment	Right to bear arms
3rd Amendment	Protection against quartering of soldiers
4th Amendment	Protection against illegal search and seizure
5th Amendment	Right to due process; protection against self-incrimination and double jeopardy
6th Amendment	Rights to a speedy trial by jury, to hear accusations and confront the accuser, to witnesses, and to counsel
7th Amendment	Right to trial by jury in civil cases
8th Amendment	Protection against cruel and unusual punishment
9th Amendment	Protects rights not enumerated in the Constitution
10th Amendment	Limits the powers of the federal government to those designated in the Constitution

A democratic system relies on having citizens who are active participants. Citizens have certain rights and responsibilities to their nation.

In a democracy, the power of the government is limited and the leaders are ultimately responsible to the people. Citizens of the United States aged eighteen and older have the right to vote, which enables them to choose leaders who will represent their interests in the government. Citizens have a responsibility to stay knowledgeable about political issues and to vote according to their conscience to choose the best leaders for the nation.

Citizens can also practice good citizenship by staying politically active, well-informed, and involved in community service and activities. Responsible citizens understand that it takes a group of people working together for a community to function effectively.

Forms of Government

Governments throughout history and around the world have taken on many different forms.

Form of Government	Description
Authoritarian	Government maintains strict control over the people
Autocracy	Rule by a single, authoritarian leader
Democracy	Rule by the people (via majority votes)
Direct democracy	The people vote directly on laws
Dictatorship	A single ruler has absolute authority and is unencumbered by a constitution
Monarchy	Government by a single, hereditary ruler
Oligarchy	Rule by a small group of people
Republic	Citizens elect representatives to make laws for them
Theocracy	Rule by a religious group
Totalitarianism	A government that has complete control over all aspects of citizens' lives and employs censorship, coercion, and oppressive means to ensure compliance

International Relations

There are diverse governments throughout the world who do not always agree on policy but must learn to coexist. Foreign policy is a government's strategy for dealing with other countries. Foreign policy includes components such as:

- Economic relationships
- Conflict
- Conflict resolution
- Measures to maintain the balance of power

- Territorial agreements
- International cooperation and agreements and their enforcement
- Distribution of resources
- Communication
- Alliances (economic or military)

Economics is a social science concerned with how goods and services are produced, bought, and sold. Students should understand fundamental economic principles, basic components of economic systems, and the relationship between economics and society.

There are two major division of economics—macroeconomics and microeconomics. **Macroeconomics** is the study of how economics works on a large scale, such as in a whole nation. **Microeconomics** is the study of economics on a smaller scale, looking at the decisions and impacts of individuals, small groups, and specific markets.

Resources are limited (**scarcity**), so people must make choices about how those resources will be allocated. On a small scale, individuals make choices about what they will buy and sell. On a larger scale, societies create economic systems that determine how goods will be produced, bought, and sold and by whom.

Economic Systems

Capitalism is a system in which property and the means of production are privately owned. What is produced, how much, and at what price is dictated by the market forces of **supply and demand**. If demand for a product is high, the supply will run low and prices will increase. If demand is low, the supply will be high and prices will decrease. The **profit motive** encourages hard work and innovation. Capitalism is also called a **market economy**. The purest form of capitalism is **laissez-faire**, in which the government takes a completely hands-off approach to the economic sector and allows market forces to regulate themselves.

Socialism is a system in which property is controlled collectively rather than individually. The purest form of socialism is **communism**, in which everything is owned in common and there is no private property and no social classes. In theory, communism eventually replaces the need for a government. In reality, however, nations that practice forms of communism tend to have very strong governments that take complete economic control. An economy in which the government has total control of the economy through centralized planning is called a **command** or a **planned economy**.

A **mixed economy** is a blend of capitalist and socialist principles, with both publicly and privately owned business operating at the same time. A **closed economy** is one

75

that is self-sufficient and cut off from outside influences, while an **open economy** allows for trade with other nations.

A **subsistence economy** is one in which people only produce that which is needed to survive.

Key Terms

Other important terms in the study of economics include:

- **Balance of trade**- a measure of a nation's exports vs. imports
- **Budget**- planning how current money will be allocated
- **Consumption**- the use of resources
- **Deflation**- an overall decrease in the price of goods and services
- **Depression**- a long period of economic decline, usually marked by inflation, high unemployment, and industrial decline
- **Exports-** goods sold to another country
- **Imports-** goods bought from another country
- **Inflation-** an overall increase in the price of goods and services
- **Profit-** the difference between revenue and cost
- **Recession-** a period of slow economic growth
- **Shortage-** when demand exceeds supply
- **Surplus-** when supply exceeds demand

Competition in the Economic Marketplace

As discussed in the previous section, prices are greatly affected by the forces of supply and demand. If a product is in high demand, supplies of that product run low and prices increase. When products are less in demand, there is a greater supply available and prices drop in an effort to sell off the excess merchandise.

Competition also plays an important role in price. Competition occurs when more than one company is selling the same or a very similar product or service. They are competing with each other for a share of the market, and in doing so, tend to lower their prices to entice customers. For this reason, competition tends to drive prices down.

When there is a lack of competition and only one seller controls all or almost all of the market share on a product or service, that is called a **monopoly**. Many governments, including the United States, put measures in place to protect consumers against monopolies, since a monopoly has the potential to drive prices up.

Economic Effects on Population, Resources and Technology

There are close relationships between economics, population, resources, and technology. Human populations are greatly affected by the availability of resources. An area must have sufficient resources to sustain its population or the society cannot survive. Where resources are scarce, people must either obtain resources from outside sources or migrate to areas with sufficient resources. In some cases, societies also work to control the population and limit its growth.

As populations grow and technology becomes more advanced, humanity has used more and more resources. As these resources are increasingly scarce, control of resources is important and the trade of resources a vital part of the global economy.

Technology has made the global economy evermore connected. Advances in transportation and communication technologies have allowed for business to be conducted in worldwide markets in ways never previously possible.

The Relationship Between Government and Economics

Different nations use different economic systems and therefore have different levels of governmental involvement in the economic sectors. A command economy gives the government complete control over economic decision-making, while a laissez-faire system allows the government no role and leaves economic decisions up to individuals and market forces. Most nations' systems are somewhere in the middle of these two extremes.

The United States is primarily a market economy but it does allow the government a degree of regulatory control. The government attempts to intervene in ways that will create a healthy, growing economic environment. Government involvement includes taxation, setting interest rates, regulating the monetary supply, regulating trade, and providing oversight.

This section covers the major eras, events, people, and movements throughout the history of the United States and the world.

Topics Addressed:

1. United States History

2. World History

3. Patterns of Human Population

Students should have an understanding of the causes and effects of the major events in the history of the United States, from its colonization to the present day.

European Exploration

Starting in the 1400s, European powers began to look to expand their influence outward. They sent explorers to find new trade routes and new lands that could be used for their natural resources. During this period, European explorers learned about the existence of the North and South American continents and began to colonize these areas, which were collectively called the New World. Part of this territory would one day become the United States.

The three main motivations for exploration of the New World were:

- Glory- the desire for personal status and to bring prestige to the home country

- God- convert native populations to Christianity

- Gold- get riches for themselves and natural resources, new trade routes, and trading partners for the home country

Students should be familiar with some of the major explorers who navigated the Americas.

Explorer	Nation of Origin	Achievements
John Cabot	Great Britain	Explored the east coast of Canada
Christopher Columbus	Italy, sailed for Spain	"Discovered" North America while looking for a western route to India
Amerigo Vespucci	Italy	The first to realize the Americas were separate continents from Asia; America is named after him
Vasco de Balboa	Spain	First to reach the Pacific by crossing Central America
Juan Ponce de Leon	Spain	First to explore Florida while searching for the Fountain of Youth
Ferdinand Magellan	Spain	First to circumnavigate the globe by sailing around the southern tip of South America
Hernan Cortez	Spain	Conquered Mexico from the Aztecs
Francisco Pizzaro	Spain	Conquered the Incan Empire
Jacques Cartier	France	Explored Canada and claimed it for France
Fernando de Soto	Spain	Discovered the Mississippi River
Francisco Coronado	Spain	Explored the American southwest
Walter Raleigh	Great Britain	Established English colonies in North America
Henry Hudson	Great Britain	Explored northeastern North America and the Arctic
James Cook	Great Britain	Explored the Pacific; discovered Hawaii

The Thirteen Colonies

The British established thirteen colonies along the east coast of what is now the United States. Within the Thirteen Colonies, there were three main regions—New England, Middle Atlantic, and the Southern Colonies. Each area developed its own unique characteristics.

Region	Colonies	Characteristics
New England Colonies	New Hampshire, Massachusetts, Rhode Island, Connecticut	• Rocky soil was poor for farming • Relied on fishing and shipping industries • Most people lived in or near towns • Major city: Boston
Middle Atlantic Colonies	New York, New Jersey, Pennsylvania, Delaware	• Good conditions for farming • The "breadbasket" of the colonies • Fur trade • Major city: Philadelphia
Southern Colonies	Maryland, Virginia, North Carolina, South Carolina, Georgia	• Plantation farming (tobacco, indigo, rice, cotton) • Slavery • More rural population • Major cities: Richmond, Charleston

After the American Revolution, these colonies would become the first thirteen states. They served as the foundation for a nation that would eventually grow to include fifty states across a vast expanse of territory.

The American Revolution and the Founding of the U.S.

The Thirteen Colonies eventually wanted to rule themselves rather than continue to be controlled by Great Britain. This resulted in the American Revolution.

Causes of the American Revolution

When the colonies were first settled, they relied heavily on help from the British. They needed British supplies, British money, the British government to keep order, and the British military for protection. Over time, as the colonies grew more established and stronger, they became more self-sufficient. They no longer relied on the British for everything. They even made their own local governments to make decisions. The less they depended on the British, the more they felt like they didn't need them anymore and that they could govern themselves.

In the late 1700s, the British found themselves in need of money after the costly French and Indian War, so they began to impose many new taxes on the colonists. These included:

- Stamp Act (1765)

- Townshend Acts (1767)

- Tea Act (1773)

- Intolerable Acts (1774)

The colonists did not have representation in the British Parliament, which levied the taxes, so they didn't think it was fair that they should be taxed. After failed attempts at negotiation and compromise, tensions escalated and eventually erupted into war—the American Revolution.

Major Events in the American Revolution

The **American Revolution** began with the **Battle of Lexington and Concord** in 1775. This was soon followed by the **Battle of Bunker Hill**.

The next summer, representatives from the colonies signed a document called the **Declaration of Independence**, which listed the reasons for the rebellion and stated that the United States was to be an independent country. It was signed on July 4, 1776.

Britain was not ready to accept American independence, however, and the war continued. While the British army was more established, better trained, and had larger numbers, the Americans had the advantage of fighting on their own familiar territory and eventually secured aid from the French. The Americans won the war with a final victory at the **Battle of Yorktown** in 1781. The war officially concluded with the signing of the Treaty of Paris in 1783.

Forming a New Nation

The new nation had to create a government for itself. The first system they tried was organized around a document called the **Articles of Confederation**. This made the new government too weak, however, and it ultimately failed.

In 1787, the Articles of Confederation were replaced with a new form of government, outlined in the **U.S. Constitution**. The Constitution set up a federal system with a three-branch national government. Revolutionary War hero George Washington was chosen as the first President of the United States.

The United States Expands

Over the course of its history, the United States made several major expansions, enlarging its land from thirteen original states to the current fifty.

The British had holdings in North America other than the Thirteen Colonies. Part of this was in Canada, and remained in British hands following the American Revolution. Some of this territory was adjacent to the Thirteen Colonies and became a part of the new United States. Originally, the Thirteen Colonies turned into the first thirteen states of the United States. The additional territory, which included lands between the Appalachian Mountains and the Mississippi River, was eventually settled. The territories each eventually applied for statehood and became Ohio, Indiana, Illinois, Alabama, Mississippi, Michigan, and Wisconsin.

The next major territorial expansion of the United States occurred in 1803 when President Thomas Jefferson bought the Louisiana Territory from France. The **Louisiana Purchase** doubled the size of the nation, adding what would eventually become Louisiana, Arkansas, Missouri, Iowa, Minnesota, North Dakota, South Dakota, Kansas, Nebraska, Oklahoma, Colorado, Wyoming, and Montana.

This major expansion gave birth to the idea that the United States should one day possess the lands all the way to the Pacific Ocean. The belief that this was the nation's God-given right became known as **Manifest Destiny**. Fueled by this spirit, the nation continued to expand.

The United States purchased Florida from Spain in 1819. In 1845, it annexed Texas, which was at the time an independent republic. The Oregon Territory was acquired in 1846. The **Mexican Cession** of 1848, which followed the Mexican-American War, resulted in the acquisition of the territories that would become California, Nevada, New Mexico, Arizona, and Utah. The **Gadsden Purchase** (1853, from Mexico) completed the territories of Arizona and New Mexico. Alaska was purchased from Russia in 1867 and Hawaii was annexed in 1898.

The Civil War and Reconstruction

The young nation soon became divided over the issue of slavery. States in the South permitted slavery while those in the North did not. The interests of the two regions were relatively balanced in Congress until new states started to be added in the western territories. Pro- and anti-slavery supporters each feared losing power in Congress and fought for the new states to join their side.

Eventually, the conflict escalated and the South seceded (left) the Union, forming the Confederate States of America. The United States, led by President Abraham Lincoln, did not accept the secession and fought the **Civil War** (1861-1865) in order to preserve the unity of the nation. In the end, the North won, the nation was reunited, and slavery was abolished with the passage of the **13th Amendment**.

The period following the Civil War was known as **Reconstruction**. During this period, the government worked to rebuild the South, which had been devastated by the war. Methods used during Reconstruction were controversial and led to continued resentment by many southerners. Following Reconstruction, African Americans, now free from slavery, found themselves subject to legal discrimination in the South, including segregation and voting restrictions. Many migrated to cities in the North.

Industrialization

In the mid-1800s, the United States became part of an international phenomenon known as the Industrial Revolution. During this period, rapid advancements were made in technology that allowed for production to change over from cottage industries to factory systems. This allowed for mass-production of goods.

The impact of the Industrial Revolution was far-reaching. Goods could now be manufactured quickly and cheaply. This led to great economic growth for the United

States. Factories provided new jobs for many people, including the nation's large influx of immigrants. All of those factory jobs also drew people into cities, leading to widespread urbanization. It also led to the homogenization of culture as people across the nation were able to access and afford the same goods. Technologies produced during the Industrial Revolution would shape the modern world.

Some negative effects of the Industrial Revolution included hazardous working conditions in factories, poor living conditions in crowded urban areas, and pollution. The Progressive Movement of the early 20th century, led by President Teddy Roosevelt, sought to put in place regulations to help solve some of these problems, including anti-monopoly laws, new economic rules and environmental regulations.

World War I

Though it initially sought neutrality, the United States became involved in World War I (1914-1918) in 1917 due to a combination of factors, including the Germans' use of unrestricted submarine warfare, the sinking of the *Lusitania*, and the Zimmerman Telegram.

The United States joined on the side of the Allied Powers and helped lead them to victory. The war ended with the Treaty of Versailles.

The Interwar Period

Following World War I, the United States once again sought isolation from the rest of the world, not wanting to be dragged into another war. For this reason, it declined to join the newly formed League of Nations.

The 1920s saw a period of economic prosperity for the United States. The decade became known as the **Roaring Twenties**. Economically, it was marked by mass consumerism, buying on credit, and the growth of the power of the stock market. Socially, this was the period when women gained the right to vote, when the automobile became popular, and when jazz music came to be.

The high period of the 1920s came to an abrupt end in 1929, when a massive stock market crash led to the **Great Depression**. A combination of factors, including excess spending, speculation, agricultural overproduction, and buying on margin led to the economic downturn. During the Great Depression, inflation and unemployment were high, banks failed, and families throughout the nation found themselves enduring economic hardship.

President Franklin D. Roosevelt alleviated some of the suffering in the Great Depression with his **New Deal** programs, which gave the government a more active role in the economy. The Great Depression did not come to an end, however, until World War II jumpstarted the economy by providing industrial jobs and demanding a high output of military goods.

World War II

When **World War II** (1939-1945) broke out in Europe, the United States tried to remain neutral. Once again, however, it was eventually pulled into the conflict. The immediate cause of the U.S. entry into World War II was the Japanese bombing of **Pearl Harbor** in 1941.

The United States joined the war on the side of the Allies and fought both in Europe against the Germans and Italians and in Asia against the Japanese. U.S. forces were able to provide necessary reinforcement to Allied troops in Europe, securing the victory on that front. After a drawn out battle in the Pacific, the United States brought the war to a swift end with the dropping of the first **atomic bombs** on the Japanese cities of Hiroshima and Nagasaki.

The war concluded with the Treaty of Paris. The **United Nations** was soon established as an international peacekeeping organization to replace the League of Nations. The United States joined as a prominent member.

The Cold War

Following World War II, Europe was devastated by the conflict, leaving two superpowers left on the world stage—the United States and the Soviet Union. The two nations had competing ideologies (capitalism vs. communism; individualism vs. collectivism) and both wished to spread their ideals to other nations. This led to rivalry. The conflict was greatly intensified by the fact that both sides had nuclear weapons. An attack by either would have had devastating global consequences, so the **Cold War** became decades of competition and threats without direct military conflict.

The two sides fought indirectly in two major **proxy wars**, in which each nation backed a side in a foreign civil war. The **Korean War** (1950-1953) saw communist North Korea, aided by the U.S.S.R., fight to take over South Korea, aided by the United States. The conflict ended in a ceasefire with no changes in boundaries. The **Vietnam War** (1956-1975) saw communist North Vietnam (along with communists in South

Vietnam called the Viet Cong), aided by the U.S.S.R., attempt to take over South Vietnam, backed by the United States. The United States eventually withdrew from the long and unpopular war, and the North won, uniting the two territories into the single communist nation of Vietnam. The Cold War came to an end in 1991 when the Soviet Union dissolved due to internal problems.

The Post-Cold War Era

The 1990s were marked by an period of economic growth and prosperity. The decade also saw the rise of the Internet Age, which has revolutionized modern society. The United States was involved in international conflicts during the 1990s, including the Persian Gulf War and Bosnia.

The early twenty-first century has been marked domestically by an economic downturn. In foreign policy, the War on Terror (in response to terrorist attacks on September 11, 2001) has shaped more than a decade of international relations. The United States has fought in long wars in Afghanistan and in Iraq.

20th Century Developments and Transformations

Technological advancements were rapid and far-reaching in the twentieth century. The wide array of innovations has changed modern society. Below is just a small sampling of the many developments of the twentieth century that have had a lasting impact.

- Communication technology- radio, television, cellular phones, computers, the internet
- Transportation technology- automobile, airplane, space travel
- Weaponry- nuclear weapons, chemical weapons

Prehistoric Societies

The earliest humans were nomadic hunter-gatherers who migrated following their food sources.

All of this changed with the **Neolithic Revolution**. During the Neolithic Revolution, people learned how to farm and domesticate animals. This provided them with a steady, non-mobile food source, which enabled them to establish permanent settlements. These settlements eventually grew into cities and whole civilizations.

River Valley Civilizations

The earliest civilizations grew up in river valleys, due to the presence of fertile soil and water available for drinking, fishing, transportation, and trade. These early civilizations laid the foundations for later societies.

Civilization	Location	Major Contributions
Mesopotamian societies (e.g. Sumer, Babylon)	Tigris and Euphrates River Valley; modern-day Iraq	• Earliest form of writing (cuneiform) • First written law code (Code of Hammurabi) • Organization into city-states • Astronomy
Egypt	Nile River Valley	• Writing system (hieroglyphics) • Paper (papyrus) • Architecture (pyramids) • Strong government, military, and monetary system • Advancements in math
Huang He (Yellow River) Valley Civilizations	China	• Civil service • Advancements in math and science
Indus Valley Civilizations	India	• Built major cities • Advancements in math and science

Classical Civilizations

After the river valley civilizations paved the way for the creation of stable societies, classical civilizations emerged that were larger and stronger than their predecessors, and they would have an enormous lasting impact on future societies. These civilizations created strong governments, expanded trade, created militaries, expanded their territories, and created unified elements of culture, including religion.

Civilization	Major Characteristics and Contributions
China	• Dynastic cycle – leaders had mandate of heaven • Elaborate bureaucracy • Religions/philosophies- Daoism and Confucianism • Advancements in math, science, and technology
Greece	• Organized into city-states • Most city-states were oligarchies but Athens was a direct democracy • Polytheistic religion • High cultural period in art, poetry, philosophy, theatre, and architecture
Rome	• Two major governmental periods- Republic and Empire • Unified law code- Twelve Tables • Extensive trade network • Advanced military • Engineering- aqueducts, road system • Polytheistic religion originally; later adopted Christianity
India	• Caste system (rigid social class structure) • Math- concept of zero, decimal system, Arabic numerals • Religions- Hinduism and Buddhism • Advancements in medicine, including the invention of plastic surgery
Mesoamerican Societies	• Major groups include the Mayas and Aztecs of Central American and the Incas of Peru • Aztecs had a strong centralized government and military • Mayas made great advancements in math and science • Incas (located in the Andes Mountains) created extensive road networks and used terrace farming

The Middle Ages

After the fall of the Roman Empire in 476 C.E., Europe lacked a strong central government and fell into a period of decentralization known as the Middle Ages, which lasted from approximately 500-1400 C.E. During the Middle Ages, smaller governments were established under feudal systems, but they lacked the power of Europe's former empires. In this vacuum of power, the Roman Catholic Church became the dominant authority in Europe and provided structure, organization, and unity.

The Renaissance and Reformation

Beginning in the mid-1400s, Europe underwent a gradual but significant change. Stronger kingdoms grew; there was a revival in arts, culture, and education; and commercial practices dramatically changed and brought great wealth to what became the major European powers. This period was known as the Renaissance or "rebirth."

During this same period, the Roman Catholic Church began to decline in power and some people began to question it. Martin Luther is credited with beginning the Protestant Reformation, in which people protested and broke away from the Catholic Church, in large part due to the church's corruption. The spread of these ideas was aided by a new invention, the printing press.

Absolutism and Revolution

Governments continued to gain strength and many monarchs in Europe practiced absolutism, in which a ruler has total authority over the nation. This was based on a theory of divine right rule, in which people believed that the monarch's right to rule was granted by God so the ruler's authority came directly from God, giving the ruler much more power.

Eventually, people began to fight back against absolutism and several nations experienced revolutions. The largest of these was the French Revolution, which lasted from 1789-1799. Following the French Revolution, Napoleon Bonaparte rose to power in France and soon expanded French territory across much of Western Europe.

Industrialization and Imperialism

In the 18th and 19th centuries, the Industrial Revolution forever changed the world economy. Prior to the Industrial Revolution, goods were largely produced in people's homes or small shops and were made by hand. The Industrial Revolution brought about mechanization and the factory system, which allowed goods to be mass produced at a lower cost. This made goods cheaper and more widely available to the general population and served to create mass culture.

Industrialization had many effects on society. Populations became much more urbanized as people moved into the cities for factory jobs. Urban living and working conditions were poor, however, and social reforms eventually had to be made.

With the economic success that industrialization brought to many nations, several of those nations, especially those in Western Europe, began to look outside their own borders for sources of raw materials and new markets. This began a period (in the late 1800s to early 1900s) of widespread imperialism, wherein strong nations took control over weaker ones for their own gain. Much of Africa and Asia was colonized this way during this period.

World War I

World War I (1914-1918) was the first truly global war. It involved nations on every continent (except Antarctica) and changed the nature of modern warfare. The long-term causes of World War I can be summarized in the acronym MAIN—militarism, alliances, imperialism, and nationalism.

- **Militarism**- Nations were building up their military personnel and weapons, both as a precautionary measure and as a sign of national prestige.

- **Alliances**- Nations began to form competing alliances. Two major alliances formed in Europe—the Tripe Alliance (Germany, Austria-Hungary, and Italy) and the Triple Entente (Great Britain, France, and Russia).

- **Imperialism**- Nations were competing for economic and political control of overseas territories.

    Nationalism- National pride was high as nations competed. Nationalist movements within nations also contributed to unrest. For example, several ethnic groups wanted independence from Austria-Hungary.

The immediate cause of World War I was the assassination of Austro-Hungarian Archduke Franz Ferdinand by a Serbian nationalist in 1914. As Austria-Hungary debated retaliation, several nations joined each side of the struggle, viewing it as an opportunity to advance their own interests, and war quickly broke out. The two sides in the war were the Allied Powers and the Central Powers.

Major Combatants in World War I

Allied Powers	Central Powers
Great Britain	Austria-Hungary
France	Germany
Russia (until 1917)	Ottoman Empire
Italy (after 1915)	Bulgaria
United States (after 1917)	

World War I included new technology and combat methods that included machine guns, airplanes, tanks, trench warfare, and submarines.

The Allied Powers won the war, which officially ended with the **Treaty of Versailles**. The treaty heavily punished Germany for its role in the war, forcing it to demilitarize and pay reparations. The **League of Nations** was established as an international peacekeeping organization but was largely ineffective, due to its inability to enforce its policies and the failure of the United States to join.

The Interwar Period

Between World War I and World War II, major events included:

- **Russian Revolution** (1917-1921)- overthrow of the Russian czar and establishment of a communist state called the Soviet Union

- **Nationalist movements** in Turkey, Iran, and Saudi Arabia

- **Spanish Civil War** (1936-1939)

- **Great Depression**- worldwide economic collapse of the 1930s

- Rise of **totalitarian** regimes in Germany (Adolf Hitler), Italy (Benito Mussolini), Spain (Francisco Franco), and the Soviet Union (Joseph Stalin)

World War II

In the 1930s, totalitarian regimes such as Germany, Italy, and the Soviet Union began to try to expand their influence outward and take over other territories. Germany invaded Czechoslovakia, Italy invaded Ethiopia, and the Soviet Union spread into Eastern Europe. Japan, too, sought territorial expansion and invaded China.

During this period, Germany, under the leadership of Hitler and the Nazi regime, perpetrated the **Holocaust**, which resulted in the death of over six million Jews and others the Nazis thought of as undesirable, including the Roma (also known as gypsies,) homosexuals, the disabled, and the mentally ill. At first, other European nations such as Britain and France practiced **appeasement**, not wanting to enter another war. This failed, however, and when Hitler invaded Poland in 1939, war broke out and many other nations joined.

Major Combatants in World War II

Allied Powers	Axis Powers
Great Britain	Germany
France	Italy
Soviet Union	Japan
United States (after 1941)	

World War II lasted from 1939 until 1945, when the United States dropped atomic bombs on Japan. The agreement that ended the war was the Treaty of Paris. The United Nations was established as an international peacekeeping organization to replace the earlier, ineffective League of Nations.

The Postwar World

Following World War II, some of the major events of the twentieth century included:

- The Cold War- a decades-long rivalry between the United States and the Soviet Union

- Communist Revolution in China (1949)

- Independence movements around the world, including India and many in Africa and the Middle East

- Ongoing Arab-Israeli conflict

- Nuclear proliferation – the worldwide spread of nuclear weapons

- Technological revolutions, including television, automobiles, computers, and the internet

Population Growth

The world population is growing, but the rate of growth has varied greatly over time. Birth and death rates, which cause populations to grow or decline, are influenced by many factors, including:

- Supplies of food, water, and other resources
- Violence
- Disease
- Medical advancements
- Technology

Patterns of Migration

The movement of groups of people is called migration. Migration takes two major forms:

1. Immigration- movement into a new area or country
2. Emigration- movement out of an area or country

Migration is caused by many factors. Factors that cause people to emigrate from their homeland are called "push factors." Factors that draw people to immigrate to a new area are called "pull factors." Here are some common ones:

Push Factors	Pull Factors
<ul><li>Warfare</li><li>Disease</li><li>Famine</li><li>Lack of opportunity</li><li>Economic struggle</li><li>Lack of social mobility</li></ul>	<ul><li>Peace</li><li>Health</li><li>Resources</li><li>Economic opportunities such as jobs</li><li>Opportunity for social mobility</li></ul>

Geography and Social Studies Inquiry

This section covers the elements of geography and its effects on human populations. It also explores research methods and tools in the social sciences.

Topics Addressed:

1. Geographic Concepts and Themes
2. Physical and Human Features of Places and Regions
3. Interaction Between Humans and the Environment
4. Patterns of Human Population
5. Using Visual Tools
6. Social Science Research, Analysis, and Interpretation

Geography is the study of the physical features of the Earth. This includes both the natural landscape and the ways that humans interact with it.

The study of geography has many uses. It helps to make sense of the world and to picture the physical relationships between people, groups and environments. Historically, it helps people understand why societies have settled where they have and why they developed in the ways that they did. It helps to understand the causes of conflicts between bot historical and contemporary groups. It can also help to plan for the future by allowing for the examination of the distribution of people and resources throughout the world.

Five Themes of Geography

The study of geography is organized into five major themes:

1. Location
   - Where places are, physically
   - Can be absolute or relative
   - Absolute location- precise location on a map, given by coordinates (e.g. New York City is located at 40.7127° N, 74.0059° W.)
   - Relative location- the location of a place with respect to other places (e.g. New York City is northwest of Philadelphia.)
2. Place
   - The human and physical characteristics of a location
3. Human-Environment Interaction
   - The way that humans relate to their geographic surroundings
4. Movement
   - The movement of people and goods around the world
5. Region
   - Geographic areas with unifying physical and/or human characteristics

The World in Spatial Terms

Spatial categories are used to divide the world into parts with common characteristics in order to better understand it.

The Earth is divided in halves called **hemispheres**. The Northern and Southern Hemispheres are divided by a line of latitude called the **equator**. The Eastern and Western Hemispheres are divided by a line of longitude called the **prime meridian**.

The largest masses on Earth are its seven **continents**—North America, South America, Europe, Asia, Africa, Australia, and Antarctica.

The largest bodies of water are called **oceans**. The world's oceans are the Atlantic, the Pacific, the Indian, the Arctic, and the Southern Oceans.

The world can also be divided into smaller units such as regions and places.

Places

Places are areas whose boundaries are man-made. These include countries, states, territories, counties, cities, towns, etc.

Regions

One way of dividing the world is into **regions**. Regions are areas that have common characteristics, both in the physical makeup of the land and in the culture of the people who live there. On the worldwide stage, some commonly identified regions include Latin America, the Middle East, and Southeast Asia.

Within the United States, the major regions are the West, the Southwest, the Midwest, the South, the Mid-Atlantic, and New England.

Climates and Biomes

Climates are long-term weather patterns for a particular area. The primary climates on Earth are:

- **Tropical**- hot and wet year-round
- **Dry**- temperature varies widely from day to night; very little precipitation

- **Temperate**- warm and wet in the summer, cool and dry in the winter

- **Continental**- found on large land masses, this climate has fairly low precipitation and temperatures can vary widely

- **Polar**- very cold; permanently frozen ground

Biomes are large areas that have distinct sets of plant and animal life that are well-adapted to the environment. Biomes are classified according to geography and climate. The major biomes are:

- **Alpine**- mountain regions that are cold and snowy

- **Chaparral**- hot and dry; landscape varies- could contain plains, hills, and/or mountains

- **Deciduous forest**- contains many trees; four distinct seasons (spring, summer, fall, winter)

- **Desert**- flat land with very little precipitation

- **Grasslands**- interior flatlands with lots of grass and other low plant life; tropical or temperate climate

- **Rainforest**- tropical climate; dense vegetation

- **Savanna**- grasslands with warm temperatures year-round with a dry and a rainy season

- **Taiga**- cold, snowy winters and warm, humid summers

- **Tundra**- very cold; little vegetation; polar climate

Geographic Terms

Students will need to know important geographic terms used to describe the Earth's characteristics.

Term	Definition	Example
Archipelago	Chain of islands	Japan
Bay	A body of water that is an inlet to a larger body of water such as an ocean or a sea	San Francisco Bay
Canal	A man-made waterway	Erie Canal
Channel	A narrow body of water that connects two other bodies of water	English Channel
Delta	Low, wet, triangular piece of land at the mouth of a river	Nile Delta
Desert	Area with little to no precipitation	Sahara Desert
Gulf	A large body of water partially enclosed by land that connects to an ocean or sea	Gulf of Mexico
Island	A piece of land surrounded on all sides by water	Cuba
Isthmus	A very narrow strip of land connecting two larger pieces of land with water on both sides	Isthmus of Panama
Lake	A body of water completely surrounded by land	Lake Ontario
Mountain	A very high rocky formation	Rocky Mountains
Peninsula	A piece of land with water on three sides	Florida
Plains	Flat, grassy lands	The Great Plains
River	A long, flowing body of water that empties into a larger body of water	The Mississippi River
Sea	A large saltwater body, smaller than an ocean	Mediterranean Sea
Valley	Low area between mountains	Death Valley

Human Effects on the Environment

Humans, more than any other creatures, have the capacity to alter their environments. Human settlements have an enormous impact on the physical systems of the Earth. One major way that humans affect the natural environment is through construction. Building transportation systems, buildings, and other structures alters the landscape and displaces the organisms that once inhabited that space.

Another way humans affect the environment is by using natural resources. Earth has a limited amount of natural resources and growing human populations and advanced technology have increased the demand for those resources over time, putting a strain on the natural environment. Along with construction and the use of natural resources also comes pollution. Human activity creates waste byproducts that can be harmful to the environment.

Environmental Effects on Humans

Likewise, physical systems affects humans and they must learn to adapt to environmental factors. Physical features influence where humans will settle, what kind of communities and industries they can build there, and how easily those communities will be able to connect with other communities. For example, because of the difficult terrain, fewer people live in mountainous regions than in lowlands. Those societies that do live in the mountains have made adaptations such as terrace farming in order to survive in that environment. These communities have historically also found themselves isolated from the outside world due to the natural barriers that the mountains create.

There are many visual tools that can aid students in understanding Social Studies content. These include maps, charts, political cartoons, photographs, illustrations, multimedia sources, and more. Students should analyze these sources carefully, checking for labels, captions, scales, and other details that can help them understand the information in the source.

Maps

One particularly important skill in Social Studies is knowing how to read and create maps. A **map** is a visual representation of a physical space. There are many types of maps, including physical maps, political maps, topographic maps, thematic maps, climate maps, historical maps, and population maps. Some key features of maps that students should know are:

- **Lines of latitude and longitude**- lines marking the distance of a location from the equator (latitude) and the prime meridian (longitude)

- **Compass rose**- symbol on a map showing the cardinal directions

- **Legend/Key**- box on a map that shows what the symbols and/or colors on a map represent

- **Scale**- Shows how distances on the map compare to real-life distances

Social Studies is a field of inquiry in which students look into past or present society, looking for answers to a question about how the world works or why a situation is as it is. Students should be encouraged to ask critical questions and to investigate the answers.

Social Studies requires students to develop many different process skills. This can include:

- Questioning
- Gathering data
- Interpreting data from a variety of source types
- Evaluating sources
- Identifying cause and effect relationships
- Comparing and contrasting
- Drawing conclusions

There is a wide variety of source material available in Social Studies. The discipline requires students to become skilled at interpreting many types of texts, including books, articles, internet resources, maps, charts, graphs, political cartoons, and more.

Students should be able to recognize the differences between primary and secondary sources and to assess any type of source for credibility. They should learn to read historical texts with the author, purpose, original intended audience, and historical context in mind.

When reading historical interpretations, students should also keep in mind that historians, too, are the product of their own time periods and cultural backgrounds and that historical analyses can reflect bias. Students must learn to distinguish fact from opinion and keep the author's context and purpose in mind when using resources.

Mathematics

Knowledge of mathematics is foundational for student success. Students develop skills in mathematical problem solving that transfer to many real world applications and career fields.

Test Structure

The Mathematics section is the largest section of Subtest II. It consists of 38 multiple choice questions (approximately 50% of the subtest). Within Mathematics, there are four major subcategories with which you must be familiar:

A. Numeration, Number Sense, and Mathematical Operations

B. Problem-Solving, Representation, and Data Analysis

C. Patterns, Algebra, and Functions

D. Geometry and Measurement

Each subcategory is divided into topics, which state the skills you must be able to demonstrate on the exam.

Numeration, Number Sense, and Mathematical Operations

This section covers number theory, the four major operations, and basic mathematical concepts which will lay the foundation for students' future mathematical learning.

Topics Addressed:

1. Number Systems and Operations
2. Factors and Multiples
3. Ratios, Proportions, and Percents
4. Probability

Basic Number Systems

There are several basic categories of numbers.

- **Natural numbers** are those numbers we typically use to count (1, 2, 3...)

- **Whole numbers** are the natural numbers and zero (0, 1, 2, 3...)

- **Integers** are whole numbers and their corresponding negatives (0.. -3, -2, -1, 0, 1, 2, 3...)

- **Fractions** are portions of integers, expressed with a numerator and a denominator

  (¼, ½, etc.)

- **Decimals** are portions of integers, expressed as numbers following a decimal point

  (0.5, 0.67, etc.)

- **Even numbers** are integers divisible by two (...-6, -4, -2, 2, 4, 6...)

- **Odd numbers** are integers not divisible by two(... -7, -5, -3, 3, 5, 7...)

- **Rational numbers** are all integers and fractions

- **Irrational numbers** are any numbers that cannot be expressed as fractions, such as an infinite, non-repeating decimal

Place Value

Place value is a way of organizing numbers based on groupings of ten. The place value in which a digit lays conveys how many groups of ten (or one hundred, or one thousand, etc.) it represents. Place value is also used in decimals.

Whole Numbers						
Millions	Hundred Thousands	Ten Thousands	Thousands	Hundreds	Tens	Units
1,000,000	100,000	10,000	1,000	100	10	1
2,478,390	2,**4**78,390	2,4**7**8,390	2,47**8**,390	2,478,**3**90	2,478,3**9**0	2,478,39**0**

Decimals					
Tenths	Hundredths	Thousandths	Ten Thousandths	Hundred Thousandths	Millionths
.1	.01	.001	.0001	.00001	.000001
.**2**37894	.2**3**7894	.23**7**894	.237**8**94	.2378**9**4	.23789**4**

The Four Basic Operations and Their Properties

The four basic operations—addition, subtraction, multiplication, and division—serve as the basis for all mathematical processes.

Addition

Addition is bringing two or more numbers (or objects) together to make a new total called a **sum**. A common method used in addition is regrouping by carrying. When adding vertically, add each place value individually, starting on the right and moving left. If any single place value sums to a number greater than 10, keep the value over 10 in that place value and carry the tens place to the next column to be added into that place value.

Example

```
  25
  18
+ 11
```

```
  25
  18
+ 11
```
First, add the ones place column.

```
   1
  25
  18
+ 11
  54
```
The sum of those numbers is 14, which is larger than 10. To regroup, write the 4 in the ones column of the answer space, and move the 1 to the tens place. It will be added in there for a total of 54.

Subtraction

Subtraction is taking numbers (or objects) away from a group to create a new total, called a **difference**. A common method used in subtraction is regrouping by borrowing. When subtracting vertically, subtract each place value individually, moving from right to left. If ever the top number (the one you are subtracting *from*) is smaller than the bottom number (the one being subtracted), you will need to borrow. To borrow, add 10 to the digit you were trying to subtract from, then subtract 1 from the next place to the left to compensate.

Example

```
  62
- 17
```

```
  62
- 17
```
Start with the ones column.

```
  12
  6̶2̶
- 17
   5
```
Notice that the 2 is not large enough to subtract the 7 from it. This means we will need to borrow.

```
5 12
  6̶2̶
- 17
  45
```
Borrow from the tens column by subtracting 1 from the top number, making the 6 into a 5. Then subtract the tens column. The answer is 45.

Multiplication

Multiplication is adding a number to itself a certain number of times. It is ultimately a shortcut to repeated addition. Multiplication quantifies equal groups of things.

The two numbers in a multiplication problem are called the multiplicand and the multiplier. The answer is called the **product**. The typical process for multiplication involves multiplying the multiplicand by each digit of the multiplier, then adding the results to get the product.

Example

```
  42
x 13
```

```
  42
x 13
 126
```
Start by multiplying the multiplicand (42) by the ones place of the multiplier. 4 x 3 = 12 and 2 x 3 =6

```
  42
x 13
 126
 420
```
Then, multiply 42 by the tens place of the multiplier, using a 0 to hold the place value in the ones.

2 x 1 = 2 and 4 x 1 = 4

```
  42
x 13
 126
+420
 546
```
Finally, add these results to get the final product of 546.

Division

Division is splitting a number into equal groups. The number being divided is the **dividend**, the number it is divided by is the **divisor**, and the answer is the **quotient**.

In division, dividing moves in place values from left to right. Any leftovers that do not divide evenly into the dividend become either a remainder, fraction, or decimal.

Example

$$5\overline{)257}$$

$$5\overline{)257}$$ with 5 above

In this example, 257 is the dividend and 5 is the divisor. Move from left to right in the place values of the dividend. 5 cannot divide into 2.

$$5\overline{)257}$$ with 5 above

Expand to the right and look at the first two digits, 25.

5 *does* divide evenly into 25 (5 times).

$$5\overline{)257}$$ with $51\ R2$ above and -5, 2 below

Now, move to the right again. 5 goes into 7 with a remainder of 2. To divide without remainders, you would add on decimal places until the division comes out evenly. In this case, the result would be 51.4

Note: There are many methods for division other than the long division shown, but the basic elements are still the same.

The Associative, Commutative and Distributive Properties

Basic operations have special properties that govern how they work and can make them easier to solve.

Property	Applies To	Description	Example
Commutative Property	Addition and Multiplication	The order of the numbers being added or multiplied does not affect final result	$1 + 3 = 3 + 1$ $2 \times 5 = 5 \times 2$
Distributive Property	Multiplication	$a(b + c) = ab + ac$ Multiplication in front of parenthesis can be distributed to each term within the parentheses.	$2(3+1) =$ $2 \times 3 + 2 \times 1 =$ $6 + 2 =$ 8 This yields the same result as $2(3+1) =$ $2(4) =$ 8
Associative Property	Addition and Multiplication	If the operations are all the same (all addition or all multiplication) the terms can be regrouped by moving the parentheses. $(a + b) + c = a + (b + c)$ $a(bc) = (ab)c$	Addition: $(1 + 2) + 3 = 3 + 3 = 6$ $1 + (2 + 3) = 1 + 5 = 6$ Multiplication: $3(4y) = 12y$ $(3 \times 4)y = 12y$

Order of Operations

When an equation has more than one of these operations in it, the operations must be performed in a certain order. The order can be remembered with the acronym PEMDAS, which stands for:

- **Parentheses-** Complete any operations enclosed within parentheses first. If more than one operation is inside the parentheses, perform the operations within the parentheses in PEMDAS order, then proceed with the operations outside the parentheses.

- **Exponents-** Deal with any exponents next.

- **Multiplication/Division-** Multiplication and division can be done in the same step as one another.

- **Addition/Subtraction-** Addition and subtraction can be done in the same step as one another.

Special Properties of Zero and One

Zero and one have their own special properties that no other numbers possess.

Properties of Zero

- *Addition property of zero-* Adding 0 to a number does not change the number's value.

  $x + 0 = x$

- *Multiplication property of zero-* Any number multiplied by 0 equals 0

  $0\,x = 0$

- *Additive inverse-* The sum of any number and its additive inverse is 0

  $x + - x = 0$

- *Powers of zero-* 0 raised to any power equals 0

  $0^x = 0$

- *Zero as a dividend-* Dividing 0 by any number results in a quotient of 0

  $0 \div x = 0$

- *Division by zero-* Dividing any number by 0 results in a quotient that is undefined

  $x \div 0 = $ undefined

Properties of One

- *Multiplication property of one-* Multiplying a number by 1 does not change the number's value.

  $1 x = x$

- *Multiplicative inverse-* The product of any number and its multiplicative inverse is 1

  $x(\frac{1}{x}) = 1$

- *Powers of one-* 1 raised to any power equals 1

  $1^x = 1$

- *Quotient of one-* Any number (other than 0) divided by itself equals 1

  $x \div x = 1$

Additive and Multiplicative Inverses

An **additive inverse** of a number is its equal opposite such that when the two are added together, they will equal 0. For example:

Number	Additive Inverse
1	-1
-25	25
x	$-x$

The **multiplicative inverse** of a number is the reciprocal of the number such that when the two are multiplied, they equal 1. For example:

Number	Multiplicative Inverse
5	1/5
1/2	2
x	$1/x$

Absolute Value

A related concept is that of **absolute value**, a number's distance from 0. Absolute value is always positive. If the number is greater than 0, it is its own absolute value. If negative, its additive inverse (the positive equivalent of itself) is its absolute value. For example:

Number	Absolute Value
5	5
-10	10
x	x
$-x$	x

Equalities and Inequalities

Equations can be classified either as equalities or inequalities. Each has its own properties and rules for operations.

An **equality** is an equation where both sides are equal and are separated by an equals sign (=). There are several properties of equalities:

- Reflexive property- Every number is equal to itself.

  $x = x$

- Symmetric property- If a number is equal to another number, then the converse is also true.

  If $x = y$ then $y = x$.

- Transitive property- If number a is equal to number b, and number b is equal to number c, then number a is also equal to number c.

  If $x = y$ and $y = z$, then $x = z$.

- Substitution property- If two numbers are equal to one another, they are interchangeable.

  If $x = y$, then $x + z = y + z$

- Property of addition, subtraction, multiplication, and division- If two numbers are equal, they will remain equal if the same number is added to or subtracted from them, or if they are multiplied or divided by the same number.

If $x = y$, then $x + z = y + z$

If $x = y$, then $x - z = y - z$

If $x = y$, then $xz = yz$

If $x = y$, then $x/z = y/z$

An **inequality** is an equation where the two sides are not necessarily equal. The two sides of the equation are separated by one of the following symbols:

- $<$ *less than*
- $>$ *greater than*
- $\leq$ *less than or equal to*
- $\geq$ *greater than or equal to*

With inequalities, operations performed to one side must be performed to the other. When adding or subtracting the same value from both sides, or when multiplying or dividing by a positive number on both sides, the inequality sign does not change. When multiplying or dividing by a negative number, the inequality sign is reversed.

Factors

Factors are whole numbers that are multiplied together to get a product.

- Example: The factors of 16 are 1, 2, 4, 8, and 16.

The processing of breaking a number down into its factors is called **factoring**.

Prime and Composite Numbers

Whole numbers can be classified by how many factors they have as either being prime or composite numbers.

- **Prime numbers** are those numbers (other than zero and one) that have only two factors—themselves and 1

  2, 3, 5, 7, 11…

- **Composite numbers** are any positive integers that are not prime, meaning they have more than two factors

  4, 6, 8, 9, 10…

Greatest Common Factor

When comparing the factors of two numbers, the largest factor that they have in common in called the **Greatest Common Factor (GCF)**.

Example:

- Factors of 20: 1, 2, **4**, 5, 10, 20
- Factors of 24: 1, 2, 3, **4**, 6, 8, 12, 24

  GCF: 4

Multiples

Multiples are the result of multiplying a number by whole numbers.

Example:

- The multiples of 4 are 4, 8, 12, 16, 20, 24...

Least Common Multiple

When comparing the multiples of two numbers, the smallest multiple that they have in common is called the **Least Common Multiple (LCM)**.

Example:

- Multiples of 3: 3, 6, 9, 12, **15**, 18, 21...
- Multiples of 5: 5, 10, **15**, 20, 25, 30...

  LCM: 15

Ratios

A **ratio** is a way to compare two numbers.

> Example: If a parent has one son and three daughters, the ratio of sons to daughters would be one to three.

A ratio can be expressed in words, as a fraction, or as two numbers separated by a colon. The ratio "one to three" is the same as "$\frac{1}{3}$" is the same as "1:3."

Proportions

A **proportion** is two ratios set equal to each other. Proportions are often expressed as two fractions with an equals sign between them.

> Example: $\frac{1}{3} = \frac{2}{6}$

Proportions that include an unknown can be solved by cross-multiplying.

> Example: The ratio of cats to dogs in a pet is 3 to 2. If there are 12 cats, how many dogs are there?
>
> $$\frac{3}{2} = \frac{12}{x}$$
>
> $3x = 12 \times 2$
>
> $3x = 24$
>
> $x = 8$
>
> There are 8 dogs in the pet store.

Percents

Percents convey a ratio out of 100. Percents are represented with a percentage symbol (%). The percentage formula is:

$$\frac{\%}{100} = \frac{part}{whole}$$

It is solved by cross-multiplying.

Probability is the likelihood of an event occurring. Probability is expressed as a quantifiable relationship between favorable outcomes and possible outcomes. It can be written as a ratio, fraction, decimal, or percent.

A **favorable outcome** is an event someone wants to happen. **Possible outcomes** are all of the events that could happen in a given situation.

Simple probability (P) is the ratio of favorable outcomes (O_f) to possible outcomes (O_p).

$$P_{event} = \frac{O_f}{O_p}$$

Example 1: *What is the probability of a coin toss landing on heads?*

When flipping a coin, there are two possible outcomes—heads or tails. The probability of getting heads is 1/2.

Example 2: *What is the probability of rolling a 5 on a die?*

When rolling a standard six-sided die, there are six possible outcomes. Rolling a 5 (the favorable outcome) is one of those possibilities. The probability of rolling a 5 is therefore 1/6.

Example 3: *Using a spinner with equal segments numbered 1-10, what is the probability of a spin landing on an even number?*

In this case, there are ten possible outcomes—landing on each of the ten segments. The favorable outcome is landing on an even number. In the set of numbers 1-10, there are five even numbers (2, 4, 6, 8, and 10). Any one of these would be a favorable outcome. The probability of landing on a even number is therefore 5/10, which reduces to 1/2.

The Fundamental Counting Principle

The **fundamental counting principle** states that if there are *m* ways to for one thing to happen and *n* ways for another thing to happen, then there are *m* x *n* ways for both to happen.

Example:
If you have 5 shirts and 3 pairs of pants, how many different outfits could you make?

5 x 3 = 15 outfits

These types of problems can also be solved using a visual aid called a **tree diagram**. A tree diagram lists all of the possible combinations of two events. The tree diagram for the example scenario above would look like this:

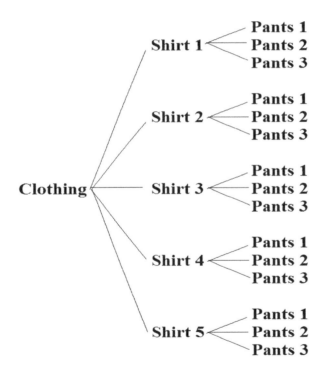

Counting all of the right-most possibilities (those farthest from the "trunk" of the tree) gives the total number of possibilities. In this case, the total is twelve possible outcomes.

Combinations

A **combination** involves choosing items (*r*) out of a group (*n*) in a situation where the order does not matter and there is no repetition.

The formula for a combination is:

$$_nC_r = \frac{n!}{(n-r)!r!}$$

This formula involves the use of **factorials**, represented by the exclamation point (!). A factorial is the product of a number and all of the counting numbers below it.

For example, 4! = 4 x 3 x 2 x 1 = 24

Example: *How many different groups of 3 students can be made from a class of 21?*

$$_nC_r = \frac{n!}{(n-r)!r!}$$

$$_{21}C_3 = \frac{21!}{(21-3)!3!}$$

$$_{21}C_3 = \frac{51090942171709440000}{18!3!}$$

$$_{21}C_3 = \frac{51090942171709440000}{(16402373705728000)(6)}$$

$$_{21}C_3 = \frac{51090942171709440000}{38414242234368000}$$

$$_{21}C_3 = 1{,}330$$

There are 1,330 possible groups.

Permutations

Permutations involve selecting items (*r*) out of a group (*n*) wherein the order *does* matter and there is no repetition. These problems involve arranging items in a certain order.

The formula for a permutation is:

$$_nP_r = \frac{n!}{(n-r)!}$$

Example: *How many different three-digit numbers can be made using only the digits 1, 3, 5, and 7?*

There are 4 digits to choose from and 3 are being selected.

$_nP_r = \frac{n!}{(n-r)!}$

$_4P_3 = \frac{4!}{(4-3)!}$

$_4P_3 = \frac{24}{1}$

$_4P_3 = 24$

There are 24 possible three-digit numbers.

Problem-Solving, Representation, and Data Analysis

This section covers problem-solving strategies and the creation and interpretation of data representations.

Topics Addressed:

1. Mathematical Reasoning and Proofs
2. Problem-Solving Strategies
3. Mathematical Language
4. Visual Models
5. Statistical Measures

Mathematical Reasoning

Reasoning refers to students' ability to hypothesize, test their theories, and draw conclusions. There are three main types of reasoning students should develop:

1. Inductive Reasoning- reasoning in which conclusions are based on observation

2. Deductive Reasoning- reasoning in which conclusions are based on the logical synthesis of prior knowledge of facts and truths

3. Adaptive Reasoning- the ability to think logically about the relationships between concepts and to adapt when problems and situations change

Mathematical Proofs

In mathematics, it is not always enough to arrive at a correct answer. Often, students will be required to give proof of their answer and their knowledge. This is where showing their work and being able to explain their answers becomes important.

At upper levels, students will begin to evaluate and create formal proofs to prove statements in areas such as logic and geometry.

There are many different methods for solving mathematical problems. No single method will be the most effective for every student on every problem. Some of the strategies students will employ include:

- Modeling

- Estimation

- Using algorithms

- Mental math

- Looking for patterns

- Calculator use

When problem-solving, it is important for students to be able to recognize the reasonableness of results. When they find a solution, they should check to see if their answer makes sense—if the number they have arrived at seems reasonable based on the parameters of the problem. This is a means of self-check.

Mathematical investigations are problems which ask students to formulate their own conjectures, test those conjectures, modify them if need be, and draw conclusions. Engaging in mathematical investigations requires students to employ critical thinking skills, to hypothesize, to collect data, to synthesize information, and to analyze and evaluate.

Mathematical problem-solving requires knowledge of such concepts as representation, variables, and arithmetic operations. In order to solve problems, students will need to be comfortable with the vocabulary associated with the arithmetic operations. This is especially important in word problems where students will need to deduce the operation necessary to solve without being able to see the symbol for the operation.

Addition	Subtraction	Multiplication	Division
Add	*Subtract*	*Multiply*	*Divide*
Sum	*Difference*	*Product*	*Quotient*
More than	*Less than*	*Total*	*Distribute*
Plus	*Minus*	*Times*	*Per*
In addition	*Diminished*		
Increased	*Decreased*		
All together	*Remove*		
Total	*Take away*		
And	*Deduct*		

Quantitative information can be displayed visually with the use of charts and graphs. There are several common types of charts and graphs with which elementary students should be familiar.

Pictographs

Pictographs use pictures or symbols to represent pieces of data. A symbol may represent one item or a key may indicate that each symbol represents more than one item. Quantities of each item are obtained by counting the symbols.

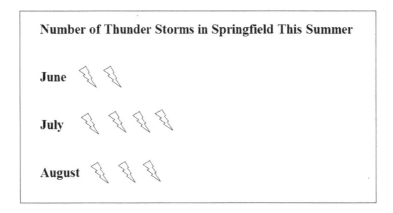

Bar Graphs

Bar graphs use bars to represent quantities. The quantity represented by each bar is obtained by reading the height of the bar.

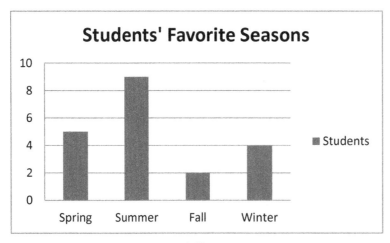

Pie Graphs

Pie graphs are used to show information in relation to a whole. The circle represents a whole and is divided into segments to represent the portions. The portions are usually shown in percentages.

Line Graphs

Line graphs use lines to connect data points and are used to show change over time.

Descriptive statistics are used to explain patterns and relationships among sets of data. The basic types of descriptive statistics include mean, median, mode, range, and frequency distribution.

Mean

Mean is another word for average. To find the mean of a set of numbers, add the numbers together and divide the sum by how many numbers there are.

Example:

Find the mean of the following set: (12, 15, 18, 20, 21)

$$\frac{12+15+18+20+21}{5} = \frac{86}{5} = 17.2$$

Median

The median of a set of numbers is the number that is in the middle of the set when they are arranged in numerical order. If there are an even number of digits, the median is found by taking the average of the two numbers that are in the center (add them and divide by 2).

Example 1: *Find the median of the following set: (34, 25, 82, 11, 47)*

In order, the set would read 11, 25, 34, 47, 82.

The number in the middle (the median) is 34.

Example 2: *Find the median of the following set: (47, 23, 24, 89, 23, 43)*

In order, the set would read 23, 23, 24, 43, 47, 89.

In the middle are 24 and 43. Take their average to find the median.

$$\frac{24+43}{2} = \frac{67}{2} = 33.5$$

Mode

The mode is the number in a set that appears the most frequently. A set can have one mode, more than one mode, or no mode.

Example: *Find the mode of the following set: (34, 52, 34, 58, 31, 19)*

> The number that appears most frequently is 34. 34 is the mode.

Range

The **range** of a set describes the span between the numbers. The range is calculated by subtracting the lowest value in the set from the highest.

Example: *Find the range of the following set: (2, 59, 27)*

> The highest number in the set is 59. The lowest number is 2.
>
> 59 – 2 = 57
>
> The range is 57.

Frequency Distribution

Frequency distribution is a representation of how many times the same event or piece of data occurs. Frequency distribution is often displayed in a table.

Example: *The scores on a recent math test were 100, 98, 95, 98, 86, 84, 80, 84, 75, 68, 80, 84, and 77. Create a table to show the frequency distribution of the scores.*

Score	Frequency
100	1
98	2
95	1
86	1
84	3
80	2
77	1
75	1
68	1

Data from a table could then be used to make a chart or graph.

Patterns, Algebra, and Functions

This section covers recognizing, creating, and predicting patterns; functions; and the application of basic algebraic concepts to solve mathematical and real world problems.

Topics Addressed:

1. Patterns in Numbers and Shapes
2. Formulas and Functions

Some mathematical investigations may require students to make, describe, and/or explore patterns.

Numerical Patterns

Numerical patterns are sets of numbers that follow a rule that governs the relationship between the numbers and dictates what number will come next in the set. Numerical patterns require students to analyze a set of numbers, discover the relationship between them, and articulate the pattern as a general rule that will work to the nth term in the series. Some examples of common number patterns are:

Pattern Name	Description	Example
Arithmetic Sequence	The same value is added each time	1, 5, 9, 13, 17, 21... (add 4 each time)
Geometric Sequence	The same value is multiplied each time	1, 3, 9, 27, 81... (multiply by 3 each time)
Squares	Square each number (n^2)	1, 4, 9, 16, 25...
Cubes	Cube each number (n^3)	1, 8, 27, 64, 125...
Fibonacci Sequence	Each number is the sum of the two numbers before it	0, 1, 1, 2, 3, 5, 8, 13, 21...
Triangular Sequence	Each number adds what would be another row to a triangle of dots $x_n = n(n+1)/2$ A numerical example of a triangular sequence:	 1, 3, 6, 10, 15, 21, 28, 36...

Shape Patterns

Patterns in shapes may involve shape, size, color, rotation, or other physical attributes of the shapes used to create a recognizable pattern. Students will be expected to articulate, predict, and create shape patterns.

Two common types of shape patterns are patterns of repetition and patterns of symmetry.

Patterns of repetition involve the repetition of elements in a predictable sequence.

Patterns of symmetry have a line of symmetry which creates a mirror image within the pattern.

Formulas

Formulas are standard equations with variables that follow specific rules and are used to solve specific types of problems. Below are several examples of fundamental algebraic formulas.

- Difference of two perfect squares

$$a^2 - b^2 = (a + b)(a - b)$$

- Distance formula- used to measure the distance between two points on a coordinate plane

$$d = \sqrt{(x_2 - x_1)^2 + (y_2 - y_1)^2}$$

- Laws of exponents

Types of Laws	Law	Example
Product Rules	$a^n \cdot a^m = a^{n+m}$	$2^2 \cdot 2^3 = 2^{2+3} = 32$
	$a^n \cdot b^n = (a \cdot b)^n$	$2^2 \cdot 3^2 = (2 \cdot 3)^2 = 36$
Quotient Rules	$a^n / a^m = a^{n-m}$	$2^5 / 2^3 = 2^{5-3} = 4$
	$a^n / b^n = (a / b)^n$	$4^3 / 2^3 = (4/2)^3 = 8$
Power Rules	$(b^n)^m = b^{n \cdot m}$	$(2^3)^4 = 2^{3 \cdot 4} = 4096$
	$^m\sqrt{(b^n)} = b^{n/m}$	$^2\sqrt{(2^4)} = 2^{4/2} = 4$
Negative Exponents	$b^{-n} = 1 / b^n$	$2^{-3} = 1/2^3 = 0.125$
Zero Rules	$b^0 = 1$	$9^0 = 1$
	$0^n = 0$, for $n>0$	$0^3 = 0$
One Rules	$b^1 = b$	$7^1 = 7$
	$1^n = 1$	$1^4 = 1$

- Midpoint formula- used to find the midpoint between two points on a coordinate plane

$$\left(\frac{(x_2 + x_1)}{2}, \frac{(y_2 + y_1)}{2}\right)$$

- Pythagorean theorem- used to find a missing length of a right triangle

$$a^2 + b^2 = c^2$$

- Quadratic formula- a method of solving a quadratic equation ($ax^2 + bx + c = 0$)

$$x = \frac{-b \pm \sqrt{b^2 - 4ac}}{2a}$$

- Slope formula- used to find the slope of a line on a coordinate plane

$$m = \frac{y_2 - y_1}{x_2 - x_1}$$

- Slope intercept formula- the equation of a straight line

$y = mx + b$ where m is the slope and b is the y-intercept

Functions

Functions are algebraic equations that have an input (x) and an output ($f(x)$). At the elementary level, functions are often expressed using tables.

Example:

Input	Output
2	5
3	6
15	18
21	24

Rule: Add 3

Geometry and Measurement

At the elementary level, students learn foundational geometric concepts as well as procedures for measuring with different unit systems and interpreting measurement data.

Topics Addressed:

1. Properties of Geometric Figures

2. Solving Problems Involving Geometric Figures

3. Measurement Systems and Tools

Points

A **point** is an exact location on a plane surface.

. P

On a coordinate plane, a point is identified by a set of coordinates, giving the x and y values of the point's location on the coordinate plane.

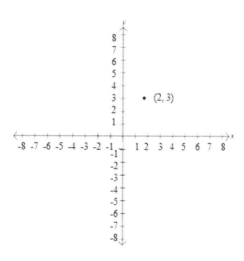

Lines, Line Segments, and Rays

A **line** is an object that is straight, thin, and infinitely long. It has arrows on both ends to show that it goes on forever in both directions.

Two special types of lines are parallel lines and perpendicular lines. **Parallel lines** are always equally spaced so that they never intersect each other.

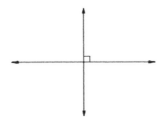

Perpendicular lines intersect at a 90º angle.

A **line segment** is a portion of a line that has two endpoints, which give it a definite length.

A ●————————————————● B

A **ray** has only one endpoint and is infinite in the other direction.

C ●————————→

Angles

An **angle** is the space formed by two rays that meet at a common endpoint. Angles are measured in degrees.

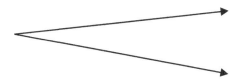

Angle Type	Definition	Example
Acute	The angle measures less than 90º	
Right	The angle measures exactly 90º	
Obtuse	The angle measures between 90º and 180º	
Straight	The angle measures exactly 180º	
Reflex	The angle measures greater than 180º	

Angles can also be described by their relationships to one another.

- **Complimentary angles** are those whose measures add up to 90º.

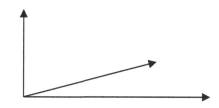

- **Supplementary angles** are those whose measures add up to 180º.

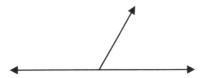

Two-Dimensional Shapes

A two-dimensional closed figure can be classified either as a polygon or a non-polygon. A **polygon** is a closed two-dimensional figure whose sides are all straight, non-overlapping line segments. A polygon is said to be **regular** if all of its sides and angles are equal and irregular if they are not. **Non-polygons** do not have sides that are all straight line segments and include such shapes as ellipses and circles. Polygons can be classified by the number of sides they have.

Name	Number of Sides
Triangle	3
Quadrilateral	4
Pentagon	5
Hexagon	6
Heptagon	7
Octagon	8
Nonagon	9
Decagon	10

Some of these categories of polygons can also be further broken down into subcategories. The most common ones elementary students will encounter are triangles and quadrilaterals. Triangles can be classified either by the types of angles they have or the length of their sides.

Triangles Classified by Angles		
Type of Triangles	**Description**	**Example**
Acute	All three angles are acute (measure less than 90º)	
Right	One angle is right (measures exactly 90º)	
Obtuse	One angle is obtuse (measures between 90º and 180º)	

Triangles Classified by Sides		
Type of Triangles	**Description**	**Example**
Equilateral	All three sides are equal in length	
Isosceles	Two sides are equal in length	
Scalene	No sides are equal in length	

Quadrilaterals can be divided into several subcategories based on characteristics such as angles, parallelism, and side length.

Quadrilateral- *four sides*	
Trapezoid- *one pair of parallel sides*	**Parallelogram-** *two pairs of equal parallel sides*
Rectangle- *four right angles*	**Rhombus--** *four equal sides*
Square - *four right angles and four equal sides*	

Three-Dimensional Shapes

A three-dimensional shape is a solid figure. There are several categories of solid figures, some of which are listed in the following chart:

Shape	Description	Example
Sphere	Round three-dimensional figure, like a ball	
Pyramid	Triangular of square base, with all other sides triangular that come together at a single point	
Rectangular prism	Six rectangular faces	
Cylinder	Two circular bases	
Cone	One circular base	
Cube	Six square faces	

Comparing Geometric Figures

Geometric figures can be compared using congruence and similarity.

Two figures are said to be **congruent** if they are exactly the same shape and size. The figures may be rotated, but the size and shape remain the same.

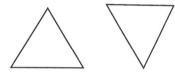

Two figures are said to be **similar** if they are the same shape (having the same angles and proportions) but different sizes.

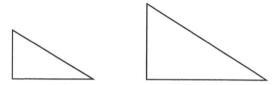

Symmetry

Symmetry creates a mirror image. A line of symmetry that passes through a shape divides the shape into two congruent halves such that the pieces are mirror images of one another. A shape can have no, one, or multiple lines of symmetry.

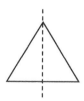

Measurements of Two-Dimensional Figures

The measure of the distance around a polygon is called the **perimeter**. The perimeter is found by adding up the lengths of all of the sides of a figure.

The distance around the outside of a circle is called the **circumference.** The circumference is found with the formula $C = \pi d$ or $C = 2\pi r$ where r is the radius and d is the diameter.

The measure of the space inside a two-dimensional figure is called the **area**.

Common Area Formulas	
Triangle	$A = \frac{1}{2} bh$
Parallelogram	$A = bh$
Rectangle	$A = lw$
Square	$A = s^2$
Circle	$A = \pi r^2$

Measurements of Three-Dimensional Figures

The measure of the **surface area** of a prism is found by adding up the areas of each of the faces. The measure of the space inside a three-dimensional object (its capacity) is called **volume**.

- Volume of a prism:

  $V = bh$ where b is the area of the base of the prism

- Volume of a pyramid or cone:

  $V = \frac{1}{3} bh$ where b is the area of the base of the object

- Volume of a sphere:

  $V = \frac{4}{3} \pi r^3$

Transformations

Transformations are a way of manipulating geometric figures by changing their positions on a coordinate plane. There are three basic types of transformations.

Name of Transformation	Description	Example
Reflection (Flip)	The transformed shape is a mirror image of the original	
Rotation (Turn)	The shape is turned on a point	
Translation (Slide)	The shape is shifted to another area on the plane but maintains its original orientation	

Students will learn to understand measurement concepts using different sets of units. The three main types of units students will encounter are nonstandard, customary, and metric units.

Nonstandard Measurement

Nonstandard measurement is how elementary students first learn to measure. The use of nonstandard units often involves measuring using small objects such as paper clips.

Customary Measurement

Customary measurement is the primary system of measurement used in the United States. There are customary units to measure length, weight, volume, temperature, and time.

Length is measured in inches, feet, yards, and miles.

- 12 inches (in. or ") = 1 foot (ft. or ')
- 36 inches = 3 feet = 1 yard (yd.)
- 5,280 feet = 1,760 yards = 1 mile (mi.)

Weight is measured in ounces, pounds, and tons.

- 16 ounces (oz.) = 1 pound (lb.)
- 1,000 pounds = 1 ton (T.)

Volume is measured in fluid ounces, cups, pints, quarts, and gallons.

- 8 fluid ounces (fl. oz.) = 1 cup (c.)
- 16 fluid ounces = 2 cups = 1 pint (pt.)
- 4 cups = 2 pints = 1 quart (qt.)
- 8 pints = 4 quarts = 1 gallon (gal.)

Temperature is measured in degrees Fahrenheit (ºF).

Time is measured in seconds, minutes, and hours.

- 60 seconds (sec.) = 1 minute (min.)

- 60 minutes = 1 hour (hr.)

Metric Measurement

The metric system of measurement is used in most of the world. It is based on units that are multiples of ten. No matter what is being measured, the units have prefixes which tell you the size of the unit relative to the others of its type.

The basic unit for each form of measurement is:

- Length- meter

- Mass- gram

- Volume- liter

Adding one of the prefixes in the chart below changes the value.

Kilo-	Hecto-	Deka-	Unit	Deci-	Centi-	Milli-
.001	.01	.1	1	10	100	1000

For example, this means that 1 gram is equal to 1000 milligrams. To convert between units in the metric system, simply use this chart to determine how many places to move the decimal.

The metric system has two scales for measuring temperature—Celsius (ºC) and Kelvin (K).

Science

Scientific knowledge is an essential part of students' academic foundation for life. Students develop skills in critical thinking, problem solving, and scientific methodology while learning about natural, physical, and chemical processes.

Test Structure

The Science section is part of Subtest II. It consists of 28 multiple choice questions (approximately 38% of the subtest). Within Science, there are three major subcategories with which you must be familiar:

A. Life Science

B. Physical and Earth Science

C. The Nature and Processes of Scientific Inquiry

Each subcategory is divided into topics, which state the skills you must be able to demonstrate on the exam.

Life Science

Life science is the study of living things on Earth, including their characteristics, biological processes, behaviors, history, and relationships.

Topics Addressed:

1. Characteristics and Processes of Organisms
2. Classification of Organisms
3. Life Cycles, Reproduction, and Heredity
4. How Species Change Over Time
5. Organisms and the Environment

Characteristics of Living Things

Living things share several common traits:

- Use energy
- Are capable of growth
- Reproduce
- Have definite life spans
- Respond and adapt to their environment
- They are made up of **cells**
- Cells are organized in the following manner:
  - **Tissue**- a group of cells
  - **Organ**- a group of tissues working together for a common purpose
  - **Organ system**- a group of organs working together
  - **Organism**- a complete living thing, made up of systems

DNA molecules are genes

Cells

Living things are made up of cells. The purposes of cells are to create energy for the organism, to create proteins, and to reproduce. Plant cells and animal cells share many similarities but plant cells contain some parts that animal cells do not.

Parts of Plant and Animal Cells	
Part	**Function**
Nucleus	Control center of the cell which contains DNA
Cytoplasm	Everything outside the nucleus
Endoplasmic reticulum	Transport system for molecules between the nucleus and the cytoplasm
Ribosomes	Make proteins
Golgi bodies	Package and transport proteins
Mitochondria	Create energy (ATP)
Vacuoles	Store food and water
Lysosomes	The digestive system of the cell; holds enzymes that are used to break down molecules
Cell membrane	Permeable boundary of the cell that allows the passage of needed

Parts Only Found in Plant Cells	
Chloroplasts	Contain chlorophyll, used in food production
Cell wall	Rigid outer structure of the cell materials in and waste out

Animal cell:

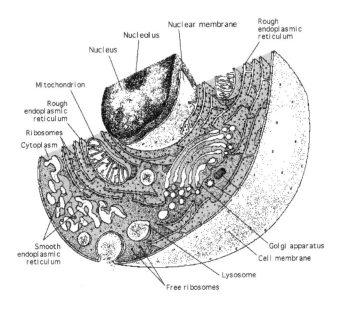

Plant cell:

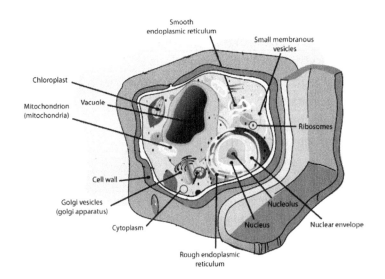

Structure of Plants

Part	Function
Roots	Hold the plant into the ground; absorb water and nutrients from the soil
Stem	Carry nutrients from the roots to the rest of the plant
Leaves	Make food for the plant through **photosynthesis**, a process by which the plant uses its chlorophyll, water, nutrients, carbon dioxide, and energy from the sun to make food and oxygen
Flower	Site of reproduction

Structure of Animals

Animals' organ systems provide the basic functions which enable them to live. While animals all possess some form of these systems, the organs they contain may differ among species. The chart below contains information about each system and provides the names of some of the human body parts for these systems.

System	Function	Contents in Humans
Digestive	Provides nutrition to the body	Mouth, tongue, esophagus, stomach, large and small intestines
Circulatory	Carries blood throughout the body	Heart, veins, arteries
Respiratory	Brings in oxygen and expels carbon dioxide	Nose, mouth, trachea, lungs
Excretory	Eliminates waste	Skin, kidneys, bladder
Nervous	Carries electrical signals from brain to the cells	Brain, nerves
Reproductive	Creates offspring	Male and female reproductive organs
Muscular and/or Skeletal	Provides structure and allows movement	Muscles, bones
Regulatory	Regulates body functions	Pancreas, thyroid, brain

There are millions of species of organisms on Earth. Scientists have come up with a way of classifying these organisms, a system called a **taxonomy**. All organisms are first classified as belonging to one of five **kingdoms**:

1. **Monera**- single-celled organisms with no cell nuclei, such as bacteria

2. **Protista**- single-celled organisms that do have cell nuclei, such as algae and protozoa

3. **Fungi**- can be single or multi-cellular; includes mushrooms, mold, lichen, and yeast

4. **Plantae**- multi-cellular plants

5. **Animalia**- multi-cellular animals

From there, each kingdom is further broken down into subcategories. The levels of the taxonomy are:

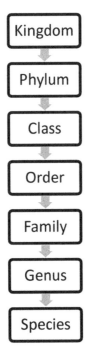

Each level groups organisms by common characteristics, with traits getting more specific the further down the classification system you go.

As an example, humans are classified as follows:

- Kingdom: animalia (animals)

- Phylum: chordata (vertebrates)

- Class: mammalia (mammals)

- Order: primates (monkeys, apes, etc.)

- Family: hominids (great apes)

- Genus: *Homo* (humans and their closest genetic ancestors)

- Species: *Homo sapiens* (modern humans)

Species can adapt to their environment, which can result in genetic change over time, resulting in the evolution of different species.

Life Cycles

One of the characteristics of a living thing is that it has a finite life span. Every organism goes through a life cycle, made up of the various stages that are common to all living things:

1. The organism comes into existence

2. Growth

3. Metamorphosis

4. Maturation

5. Reproduction

6. Death

Reproduction and Heredity

Reproduction is the creation of new organisms of the same species. Reproduction is essential for the continuation of the species. **DNA** (deoxyribonucleic acid) contains the codes for proteins, which are the building blocks of life. DNA is made up of two strands that contain **genes** that dictate traits for an organism. Groups of genes make up **chromosomes**.

Organisms reproduce using one of two types of reproduction:

1. **Asexual reproduction**- New cells are created from only one parent organism via cells that produce two identical sets of chromosomes and then split to form new cells.

2. **Sexual reproduction**- Reproduction involves two parent organisms, each of whom contribute a reproductive cell containing one set of chromosomes. The two combine to create cells with a full set of chromosomes.

Chromosomes come in pairs and each half of the pair comes with genes for each trait. The combination of these genes determine the organism's traits. Traits can be classified as either **dominant** or **recessive**.

Dominant genes are more likely to appear in an organism. Recessive genes will generally be hidden by dominant genes if dominant genes are also present.

If there are two dominant genes, the dominant trait will appear in the organism. If there is one dominant and one recessive gene, the dominant trait will appear in the organism. If both genes are recessive, the recessive trait will appear in the organism.

For example, brown eyes are a trait that is dominant over blue eyes. If each parent contributes genes for both brown (B) and blue (b) eyes, the possibilities for the child will be:

	B	b
B	BB	Bb
b	Bb	bb

If even one dominant trait (B) is present in a pair, it will appear in the organism, therefore, in three out of the four possible combinations of genes for this child (75%), the child will have brown eyes.

The way that species change over time is through biological evolution. Most of the times, offspring have genes like their parents. Occasionally, however, mistakes in the DNA duplication process result in abnormalities called mutations. Most mutations are benign and some are negative, but sometimes a mutation actually has a positive effect for the organism. A positive mutation may make it easier for the organism to survive and reproduce. When this happens, the process of natural selection makes it so that eventually, most of the members of that species will come to possess the favorable mutation.

Natural selection is the process by which those traits that are beneficial to organisms are produced and passed on in the species. Natural selection is based on a premise of the "survival of the fittest," which says that those organisms best genetically equipped to survive and reproduce will survive and will have their traits passed on. Those organisms that are weaker will eventually die off and with them, their less favorable traits.

Over time, the process of natural selection can result in significant changes to a species.

Organisms all share space on the Earth and must therefore live in cooperation in order to survive. The **biosphere** is the environment on Earth in which living things exist. It includes the land, the water, and the air.

Within the biosphere are smaller environments, known as ecosystems. An **ecosystem** is a community of organisms and their physical environment. An ecosystem requires an energy source (such as the sun), a means to convert that energy to glucose (plant life), and a means of recycling organic materials.

Ecosystems operate and transfer energy according to a cycle:

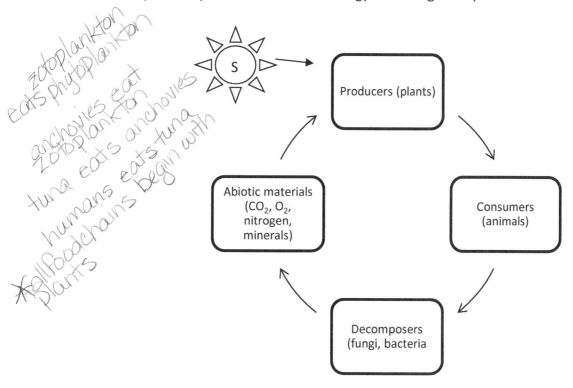

*(handwritten notes): zooplankton eats phytoplankton, anchovies eat zooplankton, tuna eats anchovies, humans eats tuna, *all foodchains begin with plants*

The Food Chain

(handwritten): Season 1/4

The way that energy moves through living things in an ecosystem is through the **food chain**. The food chain describes the order in which animals consume plants and other animals.

Plants create energy in the form of ATP through photosynthesis. They are known as **producers**. To get this energy for themselves, animals must either eat those plants (herbivores) or eat another animal (carnivore), which somewhere down the line has eaten a plant and gotten its energy.

Animals are known as **consumers** because they consume (eat) other organisms. Those who eat plants are known as primary consumers. Those who eat primary consumers are known as secondary consumers, etc. At the highest level of a food chain are those top consumers who have few natural predators and are therefore unlikely to be eaten.

Here is an example of a food chain in an ecosystem:

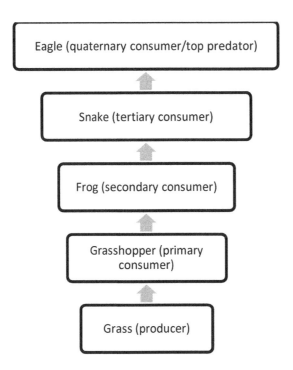

Disruptions to Ecosystems

The balance of ecosystems is delicate and can be disrupted by many causes that include:

- Interruptions in the food chain
- Depletion of any species
- Natural disasters
- Change in energy supply
- Human causes, such as pollution, deforestation, depletion of resources, mining, and radiation

Physical and Earth Science

Physical science is the study of the physical and chemical materials, processes, and forces that make up our environment. Earth science is the study of the Earth, its composition, its history, its place in the universe, and its natural processes.

Topics Addressed:

1. The Structure and Properties of Matter

2. Forces and Simple Machines

3. Forms of Energy

4. Astronomy

5. Geology

6. Earth's Atmosphere, Climates, and Weather

7. Natural Resources

Matter is the physical substance of which everything is composed. Matter comes in many different varieties and can even change forms.

The most basic unit of matter is the **atom**. An atom is made up of a center cluster of positively charged **protons** and non-charged **neutrons** called a **nucleus**, as well as outer layers of negatively charged **electrons.**

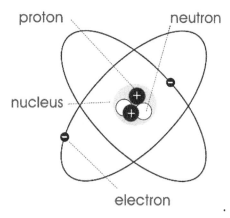

An **element** is a type of substance that cannot be broken down into different types of matter. Currently there are 114 known elements and they are listed by atomic number in the **periodic table**.

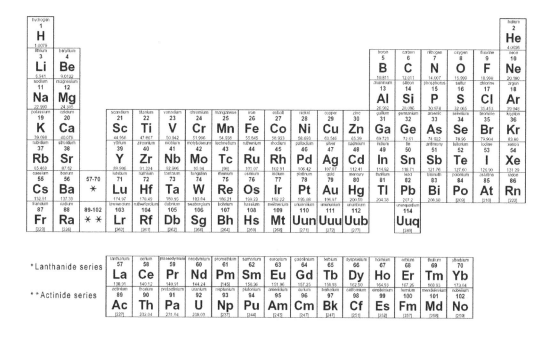

Elements combine in different ways to make up all matter. Two or more atoms combined into an electrically neutral structure are called a **molecule**. Molecules can contain atoms that are of the same element or of different elements. A **compound** is the chemical bonding of two or more different elements.

Different materials can also combine without altering their molecular composition. Two methods of combination are through mixtures and solutions. **Mixtures** occur when two unlike substances are mixed together without a chemical reaction. **Solutions** occur when one type of substance dissolves into another.

States of Matter

Matter can exist in three forms or states—solid, liquid, and gas.

- **Solids** have molecules that are relatively close together and have strong molecular forces that hold the substance into a fixed shape with a fixed volume.

- **Liquids** have weaker molecular forces than solids, which allow them to move fluidly and take on the shape of their container, while still maintaining a fixed volume.

- **Gases** have weak molecular bonds which allow the molecules to move rapidly. Gases take on both the shape and volume of their containers, as they will spread out as far as their container will allow.

Matter can change its state through changes in temperature and pressure.

From	To	Name of Change
Solid	Liquid	Melting
Solid	Gas	Sublimation
Liquid	Gas	Vaporization
Liquid	Solid	Freezing
Gas	Liquid	Condensation
Gas	Solid	Deposition

The **Law of Conservation of Matter** states that matter can be neither created nor destroyed, but it can be rearranged. Physical changes like these phase changes and chemical changes, such as the creation of compounds, are just some of the many ways that matter can be changed.

Motion

Motion is change is an object's position. The fundamental principles of motion are those found in **Newton's Laws of Motion**. His three laws are:

1. An object in motion will stay in motion and an object at rest will stay at rest until acted upon by an outside force. (**inertia**)

2. An object will move in the direction of the force that was applied to it, with an acceleration proportional to the force applied. Force = mass x acceleration

3. For every action, there is an equal and opposite reaction.

Force

Force is an influence that causes an object to undergo a change in motion. There are different types:

Type	Definition
Applied Force	Force applied directly to an object by another object or person (e.g. pushing and pulling)
Gravity	The force with which a massively large object (such as the Earth or another planet or moon) pulls other, smaller objects toward itself ; gravity on Earth pulls everything toward the Earth's center
Friction	The force exerted by an object or surface as another object slides across it
Air Resistance	Force exerted upon objects as they move through the air
Normal Force	The support force applied when an object comes is in contact with another stable object
Tension Force	Force present in a cable when pulled on both ends
Spring Force	The force a spring exerts on any object attached to it
Electromagnetic Force	A natural force that affects electrically charged particles

When the result of all forces acting on an object is zero, the object is said to be in **equilibrium** and is either at rest or is in unaccelerated motion.

Simple Machines

The most basic types of machines are known as **simple machines**. These systems perform work with very few parts.

There are six basic types of simple machines:

Simple Machine	Description	Example
Incline Plane	Used to help move things up or down by reducing the force needed by increasing the distance	
Lever	Used to lift a load using applied force and a fulcrum or pivot	
Pulley	A system that uses a wheel and a rope to make it easier to lift things	
Screw	An inclined plane wrapped around a pole that can be used for holding objects together or for lifting	
Wedge	An object with at least one slanting side resulting in a very narrow edge, used to separate or cut things	
Wheel and Axle	Allows objects to move more quickly and easily by rolling them	

Energy is defined as the ability to do work. Energy comes in several different forms, including kinetic, potential, thermal, radiant, electrical, mechanical, chemical, and nuclear. While energy cannot be created or destroyed (**Law of Conservation of Energy**) it can be transferred to another form.

Kinetic and Potential Energy

The two most basic states of energy are kinetic and potential. **Kinetic energy** is energy in motion. **Potential energy** is stored energy that can be converted to kinetic energy. An object in motion has kinetic energy, while an object at rest has potential energy.

Thermal Energy

Thermal energy (or **heat**) is the energy of a substance or system related to its temperature. Heat is caused by the vibration of molecules. The faster the vibration, the more heat will be produced.

Heat can be transferred in three major ways:

1. **Conduction**- heat transfer via a conductive material such as metal

2. **Convection**- heat transfer through the collision of liquid or gas molecules

3. **Radiation**- heat is transmitted without contact via infrared radiation

Radiant Energy

Radiant energy is the energy of electromagnetic waves such as light.

Electric Energy

Electric energy is a form of energy that is delivered or absorbed by an electrical circuit. An **electrical circuit** is the path along which an electrical current flows.

Conductors are those materials that allow electrical current to flow through them, such as metals. **Insulators** are those materials that do not allow the flow of electrical currents, such as plastic and wood.

Mechanical Energy

Mechanical energy is related to the use of machines.

Chemical Energy

Chemical energy is the energy stored in the bonds between atoms in molecules. Chemical energy contains the potential for a **chemical reaction**, wherein one set of chemical substances is transformed into another.

Nuclear Energy

Nuclear energy results from a change in the nucleus of atoms. There are two types of nuclear reactions. When nuclei are split, this is called **fission**. Fission is the type of reaction used in creating atomic bombs and nuclear reactors. The joining of nuclei is called **fusion**, which occurs in the sun and in hydrogen bombs.

Interactions Between Energy and Matter

Energy can interact with matter in a variety of ways. This includes:

- **Electricity** moves through matter (specifically, a conductor) as a current. Electricity can produce light, heat, motion, and magnetic force. Electricity can be measured in terms of voltage and amperage. **Voltage** is a measure of the amount of force in an electrical current. **Amperage** measures the strength of an electrical current as it passes through a conductor.

- **Magnetism** involves the forces exerted by magnets on other magnets. All magnets have two poles (called "North" and "South") which have opposite charges. Opposite poles attract one another, while similar poles repel.

- **Sound** moves in waves caused by the vibrations of particles. The three major characteristics of sound are pitch, amplitude, and quality. Differences in **pitch** are cause by the rate of the vibrations. The faster the vibrations, the higher the pitch. **Amplitude** is how loud a sound is, which is caused by the force used to create the sound. The greater the force that created the sound, the louder the sound will be. Sound **quality** is also known as timbre and includes other characteristics that allow the ear to distinguish between sounds of the same pitch and amplitude.

Astronomy is the study of celestial objects. Students should be familiar with the structure and processes of the major types of celestial objects in the universe, especially those found within our own solar system.

The Universe and its Origins

The Earth is just one among many bodies in the **universe**. The universe is thought to be approximately 20 billion years old. The **Big Bang Theory** states that the universe was created when a large collection of matter exploded, sending pieces of it that would become the planets, stars and other bodies expanding outward.

Galaxies

Galaxies are systems of stars. The Earth belongs to the **Milky Way Galaxy**.

Astronomers (scientists who study celestial bodies) keep track of stars by organizing them into **constellations**.

Solar Systems

Within galaxies are solar systems, which consist of planets and other bodies orbiting a star. Our **solar system** consists of eight planets that orbit around the sun in elliptical patterns.

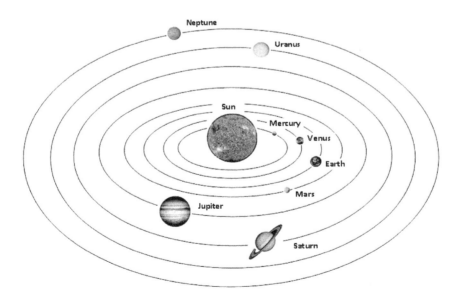

Moons

Moons revolve around planets, held in orbit by gravity. Some planets have more than one moon, but the Earth only has one, known as the Moon.

It takes the Moon 28 days to revolve around the Earth. The Moon does not give off any light of its own, but reflects light from the sun. Depending on the position of the Moon and the Earth in relationship to the sun, the Moon looks different from Earth at different times of the month. These are called the **phases of the Moon.**

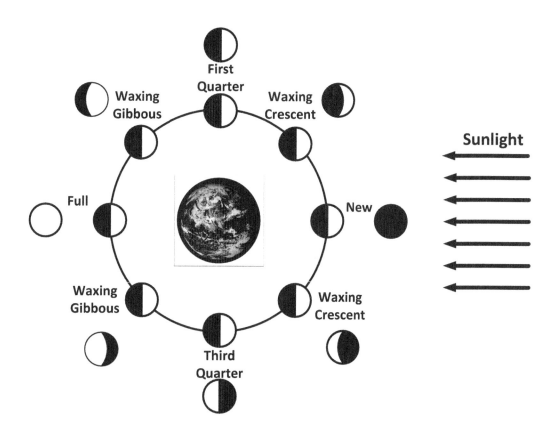

Eclipses are special events in which the sun, Moon, and Earth all line up in a direct path.

In a **solar eclipse**, the Moon is directly between the sun and the Earth and casts a shadow on the Earth's surface.

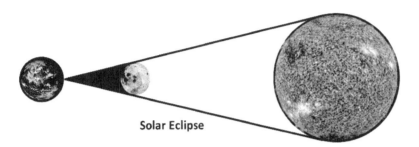

Solar Eclipse

In a **lunar eclipse**, the Earth is directly between the sun and the Moon, blocking light from hitting the Moon.

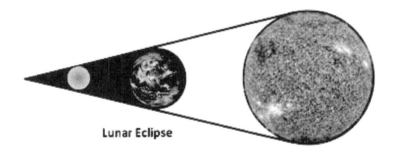

Lunar Eclipse

Other Celestial Objects

There are other objects in space besides stars, planets, and moons. Some of these include:

- **Asteroids**- large rocky objects in space; there is a large asteroid belt between Mars and Jupiter

- **Meteoroids**- smaller rocky or metallic objects travelling through space

- **Meteorites**- meteoroids that enter Earth's atmosphere

    - **Meteors** are streaks of light that trail behind meteorites as they burn in Earth's atmosphere

- **Comets**- icy bodies that form tails as they near the sun

Geology is the study of the physical composition of the Earth.

Layers of the Earth

The Earth is composed of layers, each different in its composition.

- **Inner core**- the spherical solid center of the Earth, composed largely of iron and nickel; about 700-800 miles in diameter

- **Outer core**- a layer of liquid iron and nickel about 1,400 miles thick

- **Mantle**- a layer of hot, semi-solid rock about 1,800 miles thick that has currents, causing the plates of crust on top of it to move

- **Crust**- a series of solid plates that cover the Earth's surface, ranging from 5 to 30 miles thick

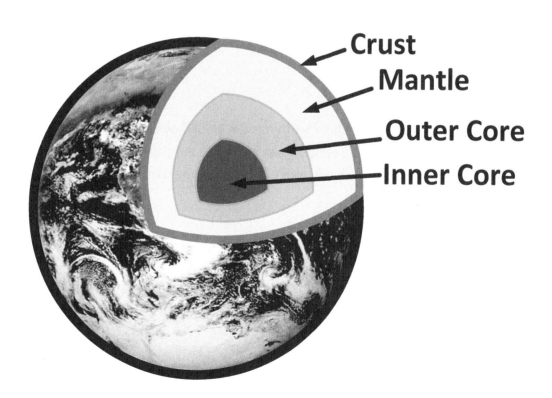

The crust consists of **continental** (land) plates and **oceanic** plates. These plates are constantly shifted atop the mantle. The movement of these plates is known as **plate tectonics**.

The boundaries between plates help to shape the Earth's surface and can cause geological events. There are three ways plates can interact at their boundaries:

Type of Boundary	Example	Results
Convergent (colliding)	→ ←	Mountains, ridges, volcanoes
Divergent (separating)	← →	Bodies of water, new crust
Transform (rubbing)	↑ ↓	Earthquakes

The Earth's History

Geological history is the study of how Earth has developed over time. The Earth is estimated to be between 4 and 5 billion years old. Over the course of its history, the Earth's landforms and life forms have undergone a great deal of change.

The Geologic Record

The **geologic record** helps scientists to learn about different parts of the Earth's history by examining layers of rock. Scientists base their findings on the **law of superposition**, which says that the oldest rocks are found at the bottom and newer rocks are found at the top. This helps scientists to date events and create a timeline of Earth's history.

The Earth's history is divided into two major time periods called eons:

Precambrian Eon	Phanerozoic Eon		
From the beginning of the Earth to the formation of life	<ul><li>From the formation of life to the present day</li><li>Divided into three eras:</li></ul>		
	Paleozoic Era	**Mesozoic Era**	**Cenozoic Era**
	<ul><li>Approx. 542-251 million years ago</li><li>Rise of early life including trilobites, shellfish, corals, sponges, fish, land plants like ferns and trees, insects, amphibians, and reptiles</li></ul>	<ul><li>Approx. 251-65 million years ago</li><li>Rise of dinosaurs, mammals, birds, and flowering plants</li><li>Also later included the extinction of dinosaurs</li></ul>	<ul><li>Approx. 65 million years ago to present day</li><li>Rise of primates, including hominids and eventually modern humans</li></ul>

Paleontology is the study of fossils. These scientists can study the origins and history of life by looking at the fossils contained within the layers of rock that compose the Earth. The evolution of life is examined in greater detail in the Life Science section.

The Processes of the Earth System

The Earth operates according to several systems and processes, all of which are interrelated and work together to create an environment in which life is sustainable.

Heat

Heat is a process that greatly affects everything else on Earth. The Earth's heat comes from:

- **Radioactivity** at the Earth's core, which is responsible for the movement of plates and thus the creation of landforms.

- **Solar energy**, which heats Earth's surface.

  o The **tilt** of the Earth on its **axis** determines the amount of direct radiation from the sun at any given point on Earth. Locations closest to the equator receive the most direct solar rays and are therefore warmer throughout the year than the poles.

  o The **rotation** of the Earth is responsible for night and day and the gain and loss of heat and sunlight that accompany those times of day.

  o The **revolution** of the Earth around the sun is responsible for the changing of the seasons.

Geological Processes

Geological processes are processes at work on the Earth's landforms. There are three major types of rocks:

Type of Rock	Description	Examples
Igneous	Formed through the cooling of magma	Granite, obsidian, pumice
Sedimentary	Formed when sediments (bits of eroded rock, sand, shells, fossils, etc.) are compressed into hard layers over time	Sandstone, limestone, shale
Metamorphic	Formerly igneous and sedimentary rocks that have morphed due to heat and pressure	Marble, quartzite, slate

These rock layers that make up the Earth's surface can change over time through forces such as weathering and erosion. **Weathering** is the breaking down of rock via natural forces such as water, ice, wind, and the sun. **Erosion** is when pieces of the weathered material are carried away via wind and water.

The **rock cycle** describes how rocks are created, changed, and destroyed.

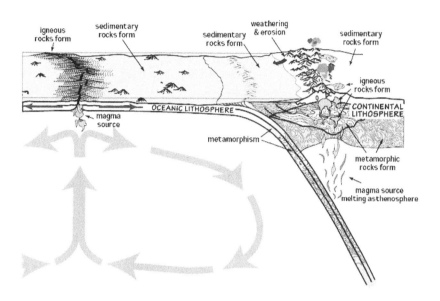

Water Cycle

The **water cycle** shows how water circulates through the Earth's surface and atmosphere.

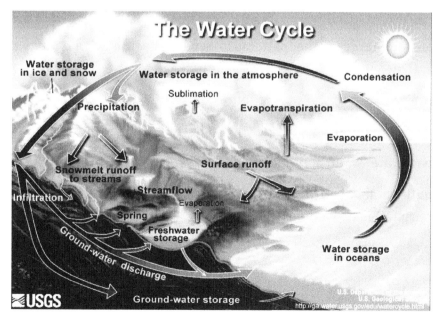

Layers of the Atmosphere

The **atmosphere** (the air above Earth) also exists in layers.

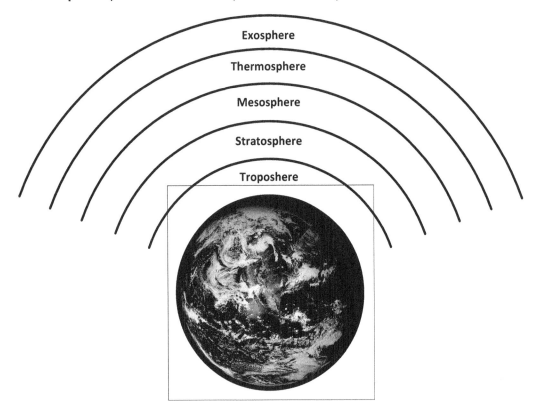

Exosphere

Thermosphere

Mesosphere

Stratosphere

Troposhere

Climates

Climates are long-term weather patterns for a particular area. The primary climates on Earth are:

- **Tropical**- hot and wet year-round

- **Dry**- temperature varies widely from day to night; very little precipitation

- **Temperate**- warm and wet in the summer, cool and dry in the winter

- **Continental**- found on large land masses, this climate has fairly low precipitation and temperatures can vary widely

- **Polar**- very cold; permanently frozen ground

Weather

Weather is the state of the atmosphere at a particular time and place, including temperature, air movement, precipitation, and humidity. The water cycle plays an enormous role in the weather, as it creates precipitation.

The weather in a particular area is greatly influenced by the season. Seasons are the four phases of the year caused by the Earth's revolution around the sun, marked by differences in weather patterns. Depending on their location on Earth, some areas experience the four seasons very distinctly, while in other areas, the weather remains more consistent.

A natural resource is a raw material found in nature that can be used by people. Natural resources are classified as renewable or non-renewable.

Renewable resources are those that replenish themselves fairly quickly so that they can be used again and again.

Non-renewable resources are finite resources that do not replenish and will eventually run out.

Renewable Resources	Non-renewable Resources
• Water • Solar energy • Wind • Biomass energy • Geothermal energy	• Fossil fuels such as oil, coal, and natural gas • Minerals • Nuclear energy

The Nature and Processes of Scientific Inquiry

This section covers how and why scientific inquiry is conducted, the connections between the sciences, and the importance of science to society.

Topics Addressed:

1. The Nature of Scientific Inquiry
2. Unifying Themes in Science
3. The Scientific Method
4. Collecting and Analyzing Scientific Data
5. Science, Technology, Mathematics, and Society

The Nature and Goals of Science

Science is the study of the natural world through observation and experimentation. There are many reasons that people undertake scientific inquiry. Two of the major motivations for scientific exploration are:

- Desire to satisfy curiosity about the world

- Seeking practical applications of science that will benefit humanity

The Changing Nature of Science

Science is a field that is constantly changing as humans learn more and more about the world. Things that were considered the "truth" 1,000 or even 100 years ago may no longer hold true as new information comes to light. Scientific knowledge is constantly being revised as new theories are tested, as scientists build upon the work of their predecessors, and as technology allows for experimentation methods that were previously unavailable.

Science is a broad subject with many branches, but there are unifying themes and elements that help to unite scientists as they share the common goal of having a better understanding of the world.

Organization

An important part of science is finding a way to organize information. There are some universal methods that scientists use to organize data from their experiments and observations. Organization refers to ways of putting data into structures. Some examples of organization include the Periodic Table and the taxonomy for organism classification. This helps to unify science because it makes it easier for scientists to communicate and share their ideas.

Systems and Cycles

A **system** is a group of related parts that are organized to create a unified whole, serving a common purpose. Some examples of systems include ecosystems, body systems, solar systems, and mechanical systems. There are two main types of systems—closed and open.

- A **closed system** does not interact with other systems. It does not allow certain types of transfers in or out of the system.

- An **open system** is one that continuously interacts with its surroundings.

A **cycle** is a series of events that repeats itself. Cycles are found throughout nature and their existence in all fields helps to unify science. Some examples of cycles are the rock cycle, the water cycle, seasons, and biochemical cycles.

Science is the process by which we gain new knowledge of how the world works. The process is one of inquiry, wherein people ask questions about the world and make observations and perform experiments in order to find the answers to those questions.

The Scientific Method

The main process used in scientific inquiry is known as the Scientific Method. This lays out the proper steps for scientific investigations.

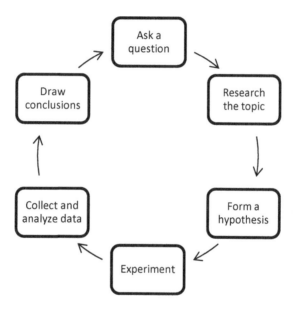

Collecting and Measuring Data

The methods used to collect data are very important in science. For scientific research to be considered reputable, the methods used to obtain the results must be reported along with the result and must be found to be honest and thorough.

Some important components of data collection include:

- Identifying and controlling variables
- Careful observation
- The accurate recording of measurement data using appropriate tools

Analyzing and Representing Data

Once data has been collected from an experiment, a scientist needs a way to show that data and then analyze it and allow it to be analyzed by others. Data representation can take many forms depending on the experiment, but may include graphs, tables, charts, and/or narration.

Analysis of the data involves looking for patterns, checking the data against the hypothesis behind the experiment, and drawing logical conclusions. In some cases, the original hypothesis may be revised and become the subject of further experimentation.

Using Resource Materials

There are many resources available to teachers in science. Teacher should use, and encourage their students to use, scholarly research on scientific topics. Resource materials can be found in books, in journals, and online. Students should be taught to evaluate the reliability of source materials. This is especially important with online resources. Research should be well-documented and come from a reputable source. Students should be encouraged to read with a critical eye.

Science is a process shared by all humanity as they try to gain knowledge of the world. It has many connections to technology, mathematics, and society as a whole. Students should be encouraged to make these connections as cross-curricular and real-world connections to content make learning more meaningful.

Science and Technology

Science and technology go hand in hand. Science is responsible for the vast array of technology we now enjoy. That advanced technology, in turn, allows science to continue and advance itself as it allows observation of phenomena and methods of experimentation never before possible.

Science and Mathematics

Science and mathematics are very closely connected. Scientists use mathematics in formulating their hypotheses, in their experiments, in gathering and recording their data, and in their analysis. Mathematical formulas are used to describe the laws of nature that science discovers and utilizes.

Science and Society

Science has far-reaching implications for society as it shapes how we understand the world and creates the technology we use on a daily basis.

Careers in science are plentiful and include a wide variety of areas, including medicine, engineering, environmental science, astronomy, geology, computer science, science education, meteorology, biochemistry, and so many more. Students should be introduced to practical applications and careers in science in order to maintain a real world connection with the content they are learning.

The Arts, Health, and Fitness

The Arts, Health, and Fitness are important components of a well-rounded education and help students to learn with both mind and body.

Test Structure

The Arts, Health, and Fitness section is part of Subtest II. It consists of 9 multiple choice questions (approximately 12% of the subtest). Within The Arts, Health, and Fitness, there are two major subcategories with which you must be familiar:

A. Basic Elements of the Arts

B. Fundamental Concepts of Health and Fitness

Each subcategory is divided into topics, which state the skills you must be able to demonstrate on the exam.

This section covers the basic terms, techniques, and processes associated with the major forms of fine arts, as well as the importance of the arts to society.

Topics Addressed:

1. Elements and Processes of Music
2. Elements and Processes of Dance
3. Elements and Processes of Drama
4. Elements and Processes of Visual Arts
5. Arts as Communication and Expression
6. Connections in the Arts

Music is an important part of childhood education. It can be played for pleasure, but it also teaches important transferrable lessons in rhyme, rhythm, repetition, and patterns. There are cognitive, linguistic, social, emotional, and physical benefits to playing music.

The basic elements of music are rhythm, melody, harmony, texture, and volume.

Rhythm

Rhythm is the beat of the music—how music connects to time. The speed of a piece of music is known as the tempo. Children can connect with rhythm through clapping, snapping, or stamping their feet with the rhythm; through dance movements; or through playing rhythm instruments like drums or tambourines.

Melody

Melody is the "tune" of a song. It is made up of different pitches caused by sound vibrations. Children can create melodies with their voices or with instruments.

Harmony

More than one note played at the same time creates harmony. Children can create harmony with their voices or with instruments.

Texture

Texture is how many different lines of music occur at the same time. Children start out learning monophony—songs with a single line. Eventually, they may learn to participate in increasingly complex textures like rounds or songs where singers and instruments play different lines.

Volume

Volume is how loud or soft music is. Children can experiment with volume in both vocal and instrumental music.

Dance is a movement activity important to children as they learn physical coordination and rhythm.

The basic elements of dance are force, space, and time.

Force

Force is the use of energy while moving.

Space

Space is the area in which the dance movement occurs. There are several types of space involved in dance:

- Shape- the way the body is positioned as it moves
- Pathway- the patterns that the body makes as it moves
- Level- the distance of the body from the ground
- Direction- which way the body moves (up, down, left, right, forward, backwards, etc.)

Time

The tempo and beat of the music and the duration of the dance.

A drama is a story acted out for an audience. Drama can be used in the classroom for story-telling, role playing, reenactment, or interpretation.

Story

The story of a drama contains the same basic elements as any other literary story—introduction, setting, rising action, conflict, climax, falling action, and conclusion. A drama can be about almost any subject. Two common forms of drama are comedy and tragedy. Comedies are usually light-hearted and have a happy ending. Tragedies have an unhappy ending, usually involving the downfall of a main character.

In most dramas, the story is written first before it is performed. The written form is called a script. In some cases, actors perform all or some actions and words that are not scripted. This is called improvisation.

Characters

Characters are played by actors. Just like in other forms of narrative, there is usually a protagonist and an antagonist.

Dialogue

Dialogue is how stories are told through drama. Dialogue consists of the spoken words of the actors.

Stage

The stage is the area used for performance. It may or may not be a raised area.

Sets and Costumes

Sometimes, sets and costumes are used to enhance dramas and make them more realistic for the audience. Sets are elements such as backdrops and furniture that help transform the stage space into the setting of the play. Costumes are the clothes, shoes, makeup, wigs, etc. that make the actors physically resemble their characters.

The visual arts allow children to experiment with expression in a variety of mediums. Examples of visual arts appropriate for the elementary level are drawing, coloring, painting, sculpture, and collage.

The basic elements of art are line, shape, color, texture, form, value, and space.

Line

In art, a line is defined as a path made by a moving point, object, or mark. Unlike in math, a line doesn't have to be straight. It can be curved, squiggly, curly, straight, wavy, jagged, zigzag, dotted, dashed, smooth, or broken. Lines can go in any direction.

Shape

A shape is a two-dimensional enclosed area. Shapes are not limited to traditional geometric shapes and may be organic or irregular.

Color

Color is derived from absorbed or reflected light. The primary colors are red, blue, and yellow. Secondary colors, formed by blending primary colors, and green, purple, and orange. Students often learn about the colors through color mixing experiments and through the color wheel.

Texture

Texture is the way something feels (if three-dimensional, called real texture) or looks like it would feel if you could touch it (if two-dimensional, called implied texture).

Form

A form is a three-dimensional object—something with height, width, and depth.

Value

Value refers to the darkness or lightness of an object. Value is created through light, shadow, shade, and tints. Shades are created by adding black to a color, while tints are created by adding white.

Space

Space is emptiness either in or around an object. Positive space is the area that a shape takes up and negative space is the area around it. Objects that appear to be in the front of a piece of art are said to be in the foreground; those in the mid-space are in the middle ground; and those that appear farthest from the viewer are said to be in the background.

The arts can be used as a means of communication and self-expression. Thoughts and feelings that may be difficult to put into words can be brought out through the creative self-expression that the arts allow.

The arts encourage self-confidence, independence, and the use of strengths and talents. They help to develop children's imaginations and promote higher order thinking skills.

The arts can easily connect to one another, to other disciplines, and to students' everyday lives. Overall, the arts have been shown to improve higher order thinking skills, self-discipline, physical skills, communication skills, concentration, memory, and cooperation.

Integrating the arts into other subjects increases success in those areas. Some examples of how to integrate the arts into other areas are:

- Music- create a song to help students remember a concept in any subject area, use music to teach rhyme, use period music to enhance understanding of historical settings
- Dance- create motions to help students remember steps or a concept in any subject, learn the dance of a particular culture or time period
- Drama- act out scenes from literary works, situations from math or science word problems, or historical events; role play; use drama to reinforce social skills
- Visual Arts- use drawings to accompany journaling; illustrate literary works, scientific processes, or historical events

Fundamental Concepts of Health and Fitness

Students will learn about the structures and processes of the human body along with how to take care of that body through nutrition, physical fitness, disease prevention, and making healthy life choices.

Topics Addressed:

1. Structures and Functions of the Human Body

2. Disease Prevention and Nutrition

3. Physical, Mental, and Emotional Health and Safety

4. Promoting Skill Development through Fitness Activities

The human body contains the following systems:

System	Function	Body Parts Involved
Digestive	Provides nutrition to the body	Mouth, tongue, esophagus, stomach, large and small intestines
Circulatory	Carries blood throughout the body	Heart, veins, arteries
Respiratory	Brings in oxygen and expels carbon dioxide	Nose, mouth, trachea, lungs
Excretory	Eliminates waste	Skin, kidneys, bladder
Nervous	Carries electrical signals from brain to the cells	Brain, nerves
Reproductive	Creates offspring	Uterus, ovaries, testes, penis
Muscular	Allows movement	Muscles
Skeletal	Provides structure and allows movement	Bones
Endocrine	Regulates body functions through hormones	Brain, glands throughout the body, pancreas
Immune	Defends the body from illness	T-cells carried by blood

Communicable Diseases

Communicable diseases are those illnesses that can be spread from person to person. Students should learn the important steps in communicable disease prevention.

Personal hygiene, such as hand washing, covering the mouth when coughing or sneezing, and general cleanliness can help prevent the spread of communicable diseases.

Some diseases are also prevented through the use of vaccinations, which help people develop a resistance to a disease by putting a small amount of an inactive virus into the person's body, allowing the immune system to create antibodies against it.

Nutrition

Nutrition tells students how to eat in a way that is healthy. Food is required to provide energy that the body needs to carry on its functions. Eating healthy foods provides the body with the best possible energy. Three basic components of food are protein, carbohydrates, and fat.

- Proteins assist with muscle growth.
- Carbohydrates provide energy.
- Fat is stored for the body to use when it doesn't get enough food.

Foods come in five basic groups—grains, meats, dairy, fruits, and vegetables. (Sweets and other innutritious foods are considered empty calories and are not a part of these food groups.) A healthy diet includes a balance of these groups. Students should also be aware of some of the adverse effects of not maintaining a nutritious diet, including obesity, heart disease, and diabetes.

Maintaining a healthy lifestyle involves more than just nutrition, exercise, or good hygiene alone. It's about making healthy choices every day that affect the whole body—physically, mentally, and emotionally.

Physical Fitness

Physical fitness is the body's overall state of physical health—its ability to effectively function during both work and leisure activities. It involves muscle strength and endurance, cardiovascular endurance, flexibility, and body mass index.

Safety

Health education also involves teaching students proper safety. This includes such concepts as etiquette and safe behavior in traffic (as a pedestrian or on a bicycle), fire safety, playground safety, emergency procedures, basic first aid, violence, and stranger safety.

Mental and Emotional Health

Students should be led to identify and express their feelings and learn to direct those feelings in appropriate ways. Students must also learn appropriate ways to interact with others, including basic social skills, negotiation skills, peer mediation, refusal skills when confronted with peer pressure, and how to identify, prevent, and cope with bullying. Students should also be familiar with mental health risks such as depression and suicide, learn the warning signs, and learn how to respond.

Drugs and Alcohol

Drugs and alcohol are substances that can be harmful to the body. Even legal drugs like medicine can be harmful if used improperly. Students should understand the classification of medicinal drugs as prescription or over-the-counter and understand the risks of improper use of even these supposedly helpful substances. Students should be aware of the various types of drugs—both legal and illegal—and their potential effects on the body.

There are three basic categories of drugs—stimulants, depressants, and hallucinogens.

Type of Drug	Examples	Effects on the Body
Stimulants	Nicotine, caffeine, cocaine, amphetamines, ecstasy, meth	Elevated mood, high followed by a crash, paranoia, restlessness, irritability
Depressants	Alcohol, heroin, morphine, codeine, barbiturates, tranquilizers, marijuana	Depressed central nervous system, slow responses, reduced pain, reduced inhibitions
Hallucinogens	LSD, PCP, psilocybin	Altered mental perception, hallucinations

There are several major types of physical skills that can be developed through physical activities.

Locomotor Skills

Locomotor skills are those skills that enable movement over distances. For children, these include such movements as walking, running, hopping, leaping, galloping, and skipping.

Non-Locomotor Skills

Non-locomotor skills are movements that do not involve travel over distances. Common non-locomotor skills for children include balance, twisting, turning, bending, and stretching.

Manipulative Skills

Manipulative skills involve using an implement such as a ball or other piece of equipment. Common manipulative skills for children include catching, throwing, carrying, kicking, and dribbling.

Body Management Skills

Body management skills require students to have the perceptual awareness and physical control necessary to be aware of the space around them and to control their physical movements within that space.

www.west.resinc.com

914 928.4192
or
800-784-4999

Practice Examination

Subtest I

Reading and Language Arts

Questions 1-3 refer to the following passage:

Whose woods these are I think I know.
His house is in the village, though;
He will not see me stopping here
To watch his woods fill up with snow.

My little horse must think it queer
To stop without a farmhouse near
Between the woods and frozen lake
The darkest evening of the year.

He gives his harness bells a shake
To ask if there is some mistake.
The only other sound's the sweep
Of easy wind and downy flake.

The woods are lovely, dark, and deep,
But I have promises to keep,
And miles to go before I sleep,
And miles to go before I sleep.
          —Robert Frost

1. Which type of stanza does this poem employ?

   A. Quatrain

   B. Couplet

   C. Sestet

   D. Quintain

2. According to the narrator, why does he not stay to watch the snow longer?

   A. His horse is anxious.

   B. He is afraid the homeowner will see him.

   C. He is afraid of the dark.

   D. He has somewhere else he needs to be.

3. The last two lines of the poem employ which literary technique?

A. Alliteration

B. Repetition

C. Free verse

D. Personification

4. "My daughter's doll" is an example of a(n)

A. dependent clause

B. independent clause

C. phrase

D. declarative sentence

5. Which of these is considered a form of drama?

A. allegory

B. puppetry

C. novel

D. parable

6. The understanding that words are made up of letters that have different sounds is known as

A. phonemic awareness

B. the alphabetic principle

C. the logographic foundation

D. syllabication

7. Which of the following is NOT an appropriate way to correct a run-on sentence?

A. Separate the two independent clauses with a semicolon.

B. Separate the two independent clauses into two separate sentences.

C. Join two independent clauses with a conjunction.

D. Separate the two independent clauses with a comma.

"Tom appeared on the sidewalk with a bucket of whitewash and a long-handled brush. He surveyed the fence, and all gladness left him and a deep melancholy settled down upon his spirit. Thirty yards of board fence nine feet high. Life to him seemed hollow, and existence but a burden. Sighing, he dipped his brush and passed it along the topmost plank; repeated the operation; did it again; compared the insignificant whitewashed streak with the far-reaching continent of unwhitewashed fence, and sat down on a tree-box discouraged."
-From *The Adventures of Tom Sawyer* by Mark Twain

8. The comparison of the "insignificant whitewashed streak" to the "far-reaching continent of unwhitewashed fence" is used to

   A. provide a precise measurement of the painted area
   B. demonstrate how hard Tom had been working
   C. emphasize the perceived enormity of Tom's task
   D. portray Tom as unintelligent

9. If a student were unfamiliar with the word "melancholy," which word(s) in the passage might provide the best context clue as to its meaning?

   A. "upon his spirit"
   B. "far-reaching"
   C. "insignificant"
   D. "gladness left him"

10. In this passage, Tom appears to be

   A. dedicated
   B. reluctant
   C. motivated
   D. inventive

11. Which of these is considered an abstract noun?

   A. Donor
   B. Money
   C. Generosity
   D. Check

12. **Protagonist and antagonist are the two main types of**

    A. settings
    B. conflicts
    C. narrators
    D. characters

13. **The purpose of an editorial is typically**

    A. to entertain
    B. to inform
    C. to persuade
    D. to teach

Question 14 refers to the following passage:

JULIET: (to Romeo) Good night, good night! parting is such sweet sorrow,
That I shall say good night till it be morrow.
    -*Romeo and Juliet* by William Shakespeare, Act 2, Scene 2

14. **The passage above is an example of**

    A. monologue
    B. soliloquoy
    C. dialogue
    D. prose

15. **Which of these is used to measure fluency?**

    A. Accuracy
    B. Rate
    C. All of the above
    D. None of the above

16. **The turning point of a story is known as the**

    A. exposition
    B. conflict
    C. setting
    D. climax

17. "Teacher picked up book off of floor." This sentence is missing

A. articles
B. verbs
C. prepositions
D. nouns

Question 18 refers to the following passage:

"Hickory, Dickory, Dock,
The mouse ran up the clock."

18. The lines above best demonstrate

A. assonance
B. alliteration
C. consonance
D. end rhyme

19. A child who writes "I herd the anamuls make lots of noyz" is exhibiting which stage of writing development?

A. Conventional spelling
B. Random letters
C. Phonetic spelling
D. Letter-like forms

20. Anne Frank's diary is a(n)

A. novel
B. sonnet
C. allegory
D. primary source

21. Which of these words does NOT contain an affix?

A. Bicycle
B. Largest
C. Start
D. Prediction

22. **Effective listening involves**

   A. focusing on the speaker
   B. paying attention to nonverbal cues
   C. responding appropriately
   D. all of the above

23. **"Please pick up the book that's _____ the desk." What type of word would best complete this sentence?**

   A. Preposition
   B. Conjunction
   C. Noun
   D. Adjective

24. **"She was as tall as a giraffe" is an example of a(n)**

   A. onomatopoeia
   B. simile
   C. metaphor
   D. foil

25. **The type of narrator that can explain the thoughts of any character is**

   A. Omniscient
   B. First person
   C. Limited omniscient
   D. Second person

26. **In the writing process, which step follows revising?**

   A. Publishing
   B. Creating a rough draft
   C. Editing
   D. Prewriting

27. While speaking, Ms. King is looking for signs that her students are listening. Which of the following non-verbal cues gives the impression of effective listening?

  A. Maintaining eye contact with Ms. King
  B. Packing up supplies in backpacks
  C. Immediately raising a hand to ask a question while Ms. King is still speaking
  D. Putting heads down on desks

28. Rhyming and segmenting are examples of

  A. phonological awareness skills
  B. concept of print
  C. decoding
  D. alphabetic principles

29. A question mark is most likely to be used in which type of sentence?

  A. Declarative
  B. Interrogative
  C. Imperative
  D. Exclamatory

30. Identify the error in the following sentence: "Lily and me went on vacation together."

  A. It is an independent clause.
  B. It is a dependent clause.
  C. It uses an object pronoun instead of a subject pronoun.
  D. It uses a subject pronoun instead of an object pronoun.

31. "Because the forecast called for rain later in the day, I brought an umbrella with me." What type of sentence is this?

  A. Simple
  B. Compound
  C. Complex
  D. Compound-complex

32. **Which of the following is NOT considered a conjunction?**

    A. But
    B. For
    C. At
    D. Or

33. **Which of the following would be the best topic sentence for a persuasive essay?**

    A. World War II was a fight between the Axis and the Allies.
    B. World War II took place between 1939 and 1945.
    C. The use of the atomic bomb during World War II was not justified.
    D. New technologies were used in World War II.

34. **Which of these skills is typically the first to develop?**

    A. Syllabication
    B. Decoding
    C. Fluency
    D. Letter-sound correspondence

35. **"Lydia was feeling sick and dragged herself out of bed energetically." Which part of this sentence should be changed for it to make sense?**

    A. Proper noun
    B. Adverb
    C. Action verb
    D. Preposition

36. **"Will you come to the party this weekend?" is an example of which type of sentence?**

    A. Interrogative
    B. Exclamatory
    C. Imperative
    D. Declarative

37. "Pretty ugly" is an example of a(n)

    A. onomatopoeia

    B. oxymoron

    C. allusion

    D. hyperbole

38. "The stars danced in the night sky" is an example of

    A. personification

    B. onomatopoeia

    C. allusion

    D. simile

39. After reading the story of the "Three Little Pigs," a student summarizes the story by saying, "The only pig whose house wasn't blown down by the wolf was the one who built his house out of bricks." This student is demonstrating

    A. evaluative comprehension

    B. literal comprehension

    C. metacognition

    D. phonological awareness

40. When evaluating media sources, an important consideration is

    A. format

    B. bias

    C. message

    D. all of the above

41. Which of these distinguishes poetry from prose?

    A. Metaphor

    B. Narrative

    C. Verse

    D. Allusion

42. **Which of these does NOT contain meter?**

    A. Blank verse
    B. Limerick
    C. Free verse
    D. Sonnet

43. **Recognition of rhyme and print awareness are components of**

    A. logographic foundation
    B. emergent literacy
    C. decoding
    D. fluency

44. **Which of these language techniques tends to be the most difficult for many second language learners to understand?**

    A. Imagery
    B. Idiom
    C. Alliteration
    D. Simile

45. **Changing "cat" to "bat" is an example of**

    A. phoneme segmentation
    B. phoneme substitution
    C. phoneme identification
    D. phoneme blending

46. **Identify the indirect object in the following sentence: "Maria loaned her book to Lauren."**

    A. Maria
    B. loaned
    C. book
    D. Lauren

47. "Manuscript," "transcription," and "descriptive" share a common

   A. prefix
   B. suffix
   C. end rhyme
   D. root word

Social Studies

48. Which of these was NOT one of the primary underlying causes for World War I?

   A. Imperialism
   B. Militarism
   C. Fascism
   D. Nationalism

49. Which of these has the longest single term length in the U.S. government?

   A. President
   B. Vice-President
   C. Representative
   D. Senator

50. Which of these was NOT one of the original Thirteen Colonies?

   A. New York
   B. New Hampshire
   C. Vermont
   D. Georgia

51. Which of these had the most direct influence on the adoption of the Thirteenth Amendment to the U.S. Constitution?

   A. The women's suffrage movement
   B. The end of Reconstruction
   C. Union victory in the Civil War
   D. Manifest Destiny

52. Which of these was NOT a direct result of the Industrial Revolution in the United States?

A. The population became more urbanized.

B. Manufactured goods became more widely available and less expensive.

C. Big businesses were subject to strict government regulations.

D. Factories employed many immigrants for low wages.

53. The caste system affected social relations in _____ for centuries.

A. China

B. India

C. Egypt

D. Iraq

54. Individual citizens have the least influence on government policy in a

A. democracy

B. republic

C. parliamentary system

D. autocracy

55. Terrace farming is an example of

A. an important agricultural technique in used in prairies

B. a way humans have adapted to their environment

C. a characteristic of river valley civilizations

D. a practice tied to religion

56. A country that exports more than it imports is said to have

A. a market economy

B. inflation

C. a favorable balance of trade

D. a shortage of consumer goods

57. Hernan Cortez, Francisco Coronado, and Henry Hudson

    A. were Founding Fathers of the United States

    B. were important leaders in the American Revolution

    C. were European explorers of the Americas

    D. were military leaders in World War II

58. When reading historical texts, students should consider

    A. original intended audience

    B. the date the document was produced

    C. author bias

    D. all of the above

59. The delta of the Mississippi River connects to what larger body of water?

    A. Gulf of Mexico

    B. Lake Michigan

    C. Pacific Ocean

    D. Missouri River

60. The region of the United States best known for its grain production is the

    A. Southwest

    B. New England

    C. Mid-Atlantic

    D. Great Plains

61. Which of these is NOT considered a reserved power under the United States Constitution?

    A. Professional licensing

    B. Establishing schools

    C. Levying an income tax

    D. Marriage laws

62. The immediate cause of U.S. entry into World War II was

A. the sinking of the Lusitania

B. the Zimmerman telegram

C. the use of the atomic bomb

D. the bombing of Pearl Harbor

63. A student looking for the elevation of a mountain should use which type of map?

A. Political

B. Topographic

C. Climate

D. Historical

64. The United States' first attempt at a national government was

A. the Constitution

B. the Declaration of Independence

C. the Articles of Confederation

D. the Bill of Rights

65. The earliest civilization on the Indian subcontinent formed along which river?

A. Huang He

B. Tigris

C. Euphrates

D. Indus

66. The New Deal was a response to

A. severe economic downturn in the 1930s

B. the pursuit of equal rights for African-Americans

C. Soviet aggression during the Cold War

D. the bombing of Pearl Harbor

67. **Confucianism was a philosophy that originated in**

    A. India
    B. China
    C. Greece
    D. Rome

68. **Which of these had the most significant impact on the size of the United States?**

    A. Louisiana Purchase
    B. Gadsden Purchase
    C. Mexican Cession
    D. Seward's Folly

69. **One result of the Neolithic Revolution was**

    A. a reliance on hunting and gathering for food
    B. the adoption of a nomadic lifestyle
    C. the development of permanent settlements
    D. a decrease in trade between people groups

70. **The 1st Amendment includes all of the following EXCEPT**

    A. freedom of speech
    B. the right to peacefully assemble
    C. the right to petition the government
    D. the right to bear arms

71. **Two of the main causes of the Civil War were**

    A. slavery and states' rights
    B. boundary disputes and states' rights
    C. slavery and taxation
    D. taxation and boundary disputes

72. In a laissez-faire system, economics are driven by

    A. government planning

    B. collective decision-making

    C. market forces

    D. regulatory action

73. Hawaii is an example of a(n)

    A. peninsula

    B. inlet

    C. archipelago

    D. country

74. One advantage the American troops had over the British in the American Revolution was

    A. more skilled soldiers

    B. better weaponry

    C. familiarity with the landscape

    D. larger numbers of troops

75. A society that produces only what it needs for survival has a

    A. planned economy

    B. socialist economy

    C. subsistence economy

    D. open economy

Subtest II

Mathematics

1. $a^2 \bullet a^3 =$

    A. a^6
    B. a^5
    C. a^{-1}
    D. $a^{2/3}$

2. There were 25 questions on a spelling test. If Kristen got 21 of them correct, what was her score expressed as a percentage?

    A. 21%
    B. 0.84
    C. 0.96
    D. 0.74

3. For lunch on Wednesday, students have a choice of pizza or a peanut butter and jelly sandwich. For a drink, they can choose milk, chocolate milk, orange juice, or apple juice. How many combinations of main dishes and drinks are possible?

    A. 6
    B. 4
    C. 8
    D. 12

4. $3 + 4(1+3)^2 =$

    A. 67.0
    B. 112.0
    C. 100.0
    D. 13.0

5. The greatest common factor (GCF) of 15 and 18 is

   A. 3
   B. 90
   C. 5
   D. 18

6. What is the absolute value of -10?

   A. 10
   B. -10
   C. 1/10
   D. 1

7. The product of two numbers is 12. The difference of these numbers is 4. What is the larger of the two numbers?

   A. 4
   B. 6
   C. 12
   D. 3

8. The additive inverse of 4 is

   A. 1/4
   B. 1
   C. 4
   D. -4

9. A store buys t-shirts from the manufacturer in cases of 25 for $50. They sell the shirts for a price of $8 each. How much of a profit will the store make on the sale of 80 shirts?

   A. $480
   B. $640
   C. $590
   D. $30

10. To solve $2(5 + 3)^2 - 10$, the first step would be to

   A. Multiply 2 by 5
   B. Square the 3
   C. Add 5 and 3
   D. Subtract 10

11. Which of these numbers is the smallest in value?

   A. .39
   B. .317
   C. .3564
   D. .4

12. Two lines that never intersect are

   A. perpendicular
   B. complementary
   C. parallel
   D. supplementary

13. $x^0 =$

   A. x
   B. -x
   C. 1
   D. 0

14. The school store sells notebooks and pencils. The ratio of sales today was 2 notebooks to 3 pencils. If the store sold 6 notebooks today, how many pencils did they sell?

   A. 3
   B. 9
   C. 6
   D. 12

15. Line A contains the points (2, 4) and (4, 6). What is the slope of the line?

   A. 1
   B. 2
   C. -1
   D. 1/2

16. The area of a right triangle whose sides measure 3 cm, 5 cm, and 4 cm is

   A. 6
   B. 7.5
   C. 10
   D. 12

17. 1, 4, 9, 16, 25... What is the next number in this sequence?

   A. 29
   B. 39
   C. 36
   D. 44

18. Which of the following best illustrates the commutative property?

   A. 4 + 2 = 2 + 4
   B. (2 + 4) + 3 = 2 + (4 + 3)
   C. 2(4 + 3) = (2 * 4) + (2 * 3)
   D. 4 − 2 = 2 − 4

19. What is the least common multiple (LCM) of 4 and 5?

   A. 20
   B. 5
   C. 1
   D. 45

20. Mrs. Nelson's class is 72% male. If there are 25 students in the class, how many students are females?

  A. 18
  B. 10
  C. 7
  D. 17

21. On a recent test, five friends had scores of 88, 92, 76, 94, and 80. What was their median score?

  A. 86
  B. 88
  C. 94
  D. 90

22. On a recent test, five friends had scores of 88, 92, 76, 94, and 80. What was the mean of their scores?

  A. 84
  B. 86
  C. 88
  D. 18

23. Solve for x. -4x < 16

  A. x > -4
  B. x < -4
  C. x < 4
  D. x > 4

24. An angle that measures 100° is considered

  A. acute
  B. obtuse
  C. straight
  D. right

Question 25 refers to the chart below.

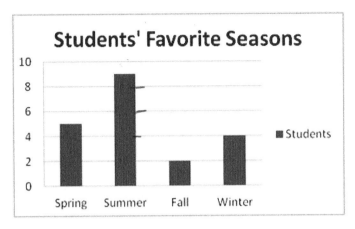

25. **How many more students like summer than fall?**

A. 7.0

B. 11.0

C. 8.0

D. 3.0

26. **2 is the only even number that is also**

A. rational

B. prime

C. natural

D. irrational

27. **One of the angles in an equilateral triangle has a measure of**

A. 90°

B. 30°

C. 60°

D. 45°

28. **The Pythagorean Theorem is used to find**

A. the slope of a line

B. the volume of a cylinder

C. the sides of a right triangle

D. the midpoint of a line segment

29. Which of the following is NOT a factor of 16?

    A. 16
    B. 32
    C. 8
    D. 2

30. Which of these fractions is equal to 0.875?

    A. 9/10
    B. 7/8
    C. 6/7
    D. 11/12

31. Which of the following would yield a result that is undefined?

    A. 12 ÷ 0
    B. 10 * 0
    C. 0 ÷ 11
    D. 5 * 0

32. Which of these numbers is NOT equivalent to the others?

    A. 1/2
    B. 0.5
    C. 2/6
    D. 0.50

33. A quadrilateral with only one pair of parallel sides can be classified as a

    A. trapezoid
    B. parallelogram
    C. rhombus
    D. rectangle

34. Using a spinner with equal segments numbered 1-6, what is the probability of a spin landing on an even number?

    A. 1/6
    B. 1/3
    C. 5/6
    D. 1/2

35. The set {1, 4, 16, 64) is what type of sequence?

    A. Arithmetic – adding or subtracting
    B. Geometric – multiply by 1 number Ex. 4
    C. Triangular – Know how to do
    D. Fibonacci – adding to previous number

36. Which of the following is does NOT describe the number 98?

    A. Real
    B. Rational
    C. Prime 1×7
    D. Composite

37. If a car travels at 55 mph, how far will the car travel in 2 hours and 30 minutes?

    A. 140 miles
    B. 175 miles
    C. 12,650 miles
    D. 137.5 miles

38. The multiples of 6 include

    A. 1, 2, and 3
    B. 3, 6, and 9
    C. 6, 12, and 18
    D. .6, 6, and 66

Science

39. **The outermost layer of the Earth is called the**

    A. outer core

    B. mantle

    C. inner core

    D. crust

40. **The food chain describes the**

    A. method of energy transfer through an ecosystem

    B. ratio of producers to consumers in an ecosystem

    C. way that food moves through the digestive system

    D. nutritional value of basic food groups

41. **Light is blocked from hitting the Moon during a**

    A. lunar eclipse

    B. solar eclipse

    C. meteor shower

    D. Moon phase

42. **Which of the following requires chemical bonding of its different component parts?**

    A. Mixture

    B. Element

    C. Solution

    D. Compound

43. **Which of these objects would make the best conductor?**

    A. A wooden rod

    B. A plastic spring

    C. A rubber tire

    D. A wire coat hanger

44. The speed of vibrations has the most influence on a sound's

    A. pitch
    B. amplitude
    C. timbre
    D. quality

45. Which of these is NOT a required step in the Scientific Method?

    A. Formulating a hypothesis
    B. Drawing conclusions
    C. Data collection
    D. Peer review of results

46. Which resource would be most useful in finding the atomic weight of an element?

    A. An almanac
    B. A periodic table
    C. An atlas
    D. A thesaurus

47. The amount of solar radiation a location receives is influenced by

    A. the longitude of the location
    B. the position of the Moon
    C. the tilt of the Earth
    D. Plate tectonics

48. The planet closest to the sun is

    A. Earth
    B. Venus
    C. Mercury
    D. Neptune

49. Natural selection contributes to biological evolution by

    A. ensuring that mutations favorable for survival are passed down through reproduction

    B. eliminating all mutations from the gene pool

    C. providing a means for weaker organisms to survive and reproduce

    D. ensuring that only dominant traits can be genetically inherited

50. Meteorites are found

    A. within the Earth's atmosphere

    B. in the asteroid belt

    C. near the sun

    D. nowhere in this solar system

51. The idea that an object in motion will stay in motion unless acted upon by an outside force is known as

    A. sublimation

    B. velocity

    C. inertia

    D. friction

52. Weather is most directly influenced by

    A. the rock cycle

    B. the water cycle

    C. the Moon

    D. Earth's rotation on its axis

53. The nucleus of an animal cell

    A. produces chlorophyll

    B. is surrounded by a rigid wall

    C. contains DNA

    D. All of the above

54. The overall charge of the nucleus of an atom is

   A. negative

   B. positive

   C. neutral

   D. dependent on the element

55. Which simple machine would be most useful for moving an object across a long horizontal distance?

   A. Pulley

   B. Lever

   C. Wedge

   D. Wheel and axle

56. Which of the following is NOT a characteristic of all living things?

   A. Made of cells

   B. Have definite life spans

   C. Use energy

   D. Sexual reproduction

57. Condensation involves a phase change from

   A. solid to liquid

   B. gas to liquid

   C. liquid to gas

   D. gas to solid

58. Human beings belong to the taxonomic kingdom of

   A. protista

   B. animalia

   C. plantae

   D. monera

59. The North Pole of a magnet will repel which pole of another magnet?

    A. North
    B. South
    C. East
    D. West

60. Which of these types of water movement in the water cycle does NOT involve a phase change?

    A. Melting
    B. Surface run-off
    C. Transpiration
    D. Evaporation

61. One result of convergent plates is

    A. the creation of new crust
    B. the creation of new bodies of water
    C. the creation of volcanoes
    D. the separation of continental and oceanic plates

62. Animal and plant cells both contain all of the following EXCEPT

    A. mitochondria
    B. chloroplasts
    C. nucleus
    D. cytoplasm

63. If two parents display the same recessive trait for eye color, the chances of the offspring also displaying the recessive trait are

    A. 0%
    B. 25%
    C. 75%
    D. 100%

64. The least dense state of matter is

   A. gas
   B. liquid
   C. solid
   D. plasma

65. The force present in a wire, cable, or cord when forces pull on both ends is known as

   A. normal force
   B. gravity
   C. tension force
   D. air resistance

66. Fission involves

   A. the joining of atomic nuclei
   B. the splitting of atomic nuclei
   C. the destruction of energy
   D. the creation of energy

The Arts, Health, and Fitness

67. Which of the following helps reduce the risk of disease?

   A. Proper nutrition
   B. Vaccination
   C. Personal hygiene
   D. All of the above

68. Shade and tint are primarily used in art to show

   A. value
   B. shape
   C. form
   D. texture

69. The human body system responsible for the transport of blood is the

    A. respiratory system

    B. musculoskeletal system

    C. circulatory system

    D. nervous system

70. Which of these activities would best support the development of non-locomotor skills?

    A. Galloping across the room

    B. Kicking a soccer ball into a goal

    C. Standing on one foot for one minute

    D. Dribbling a basketball

71. In dance, which of these is NOT considered an element of space?

    A. Direction

    B. Level

    C. Force

    D. Pathway

72. The common effects of stimulants include all of the following EXCEPT

    A. a high followed by a crash

    B. slowed responses

    C. irritability

    D. restlessness

73. In dramatic literature, a comedy is best described as

    A. a play whose main character meets an unfortunate ending

    B. a play without a central conflict

    C. a play that is funny

    D. a play with a happy ending for the main character

74. Tempo is most closely related to which element of music?

    A. Melody

    B. Texture

    C. Rhythm

    D. Volume

75. Which of these is NOT considered a locomotor skill?

    A. Running

    B. Throwing

    C. Sliding

    D. Skipping

Answers and Explanations

1. A

Each stanza contains four lines, which makes it a quatrain.

2. D

The last quatrain tells why the narrator moves on. He has made promises to someone that require him to continue to travel many more miles.

3. B

The last two lines are identical and make use of repetition.

4. C

Since this group of words contains no verb, it can only be classified as a phrase.

5. B

Puppetry is a form of drama usually intended for a children's audience. It uses dialogue to convey the story.

6. B

The alphabetic principle is the understanding that words are made up of letters that have different sounds.

7. D

Commas cannot be used to correct run-on sentences.

8. C

The comparison of how little fence Tom has painted compared with the unpainted fence ahead helps to show how large and daunting Tom found this task to be.

9. D

"Gladness left him" proceeds "melancholy" and sets gladness up as the opposite of melancholy. As the gladness left, melancholy (sadness) took its place.

10. B

Tom is very discouraged by the prospect of painting the whole fence and is very reluctant to do so.

11. C

An abstract noun refers to an idea or concept rather than a concrete person, place, or object.

12. D

A protagonist is the main character or hero. An antagonist works against the protagonist.

13. C

Editorials are opinion pieces and are a form of persuasive writing.

14. C

In this scene from a play by William Shakespeare, one character is speaking directly to another. This is called dialogue.

15. C

Both rate and accuracy are measures of the fluency of reading.

16. D

The climax of a story is where the conflict reaches a head and the story has its turning point.

17. A

The sentence is missing articles such as "a" or "the."

18. C

Consonance is the repetition of consonant sounds anywhere within the words.

19. C

These words are written out like they sound (phonetically) instead of with correct spelling.

20. D

A diary is a type of primary source, which is a firsthand account of events from a person who witnessed them.

21. C

Affixes are prefixes and suffixes added to the beginning or end of base words to change their meaning.

22. D

All of these actions are important components of active listening.

23. A

This sentence requires a preposition such as "on" or "under."

24. B

A simile is a comparison that uses "like" or "as."

25. A

An omniscient narrator is able to describe the thoughts of any character. First person narration is in an "I" voice, while second person uses "you." Limited omniscient is a third person narrator who can only convey the inner thoughts of one character.

26. C

Revising is making changes to content. This step is followed by editing, which is correcting mechanical issues.

27. B

Eye contact helps a speaker to know that he or she has the audience members' focus.

28. A

Phonological awareness is the understanding that words are made up of sound units. Rhyming and segmenting are two of its associated skills.

29. B

Interrogative sentences ask a question and end with a question mark.

30. C

The sentence should read "Lily and I went on vacation together."

31. C

A complex sentence contains one dependent and one independent clause.

32. C

"At" is a preposition.

33. C

A persuasive essay is one in which the author tries to convince the reader of a certain point of view. The only one of these sentences that expresses an opinion rather than a fact is C.

34. D

Letter-sound correspondence is the knowledge of the sounds that are associated with each letter of the alphabet. This is essential before any of the other skills can develop.

35. B

The adverb "energetically" does not make sense with the rest of the sentence.

36. A

Interrogative sentences ask questions.

37. B

An oxymoron is a phrase that combines two words with opposite meanings.

38. A

Personification is attributing human characteristics to a non-human object, such as stars dancing, which is a human action.

39. B

Literal comprehension means that the student understood what happened in the story. Critical comprehension would involve analyzing the story for deeper meanings.

40. D

All of these are important considerations when evaluating media sources.

41. C

Poetry is writing that is in verse, while prose is not written in verse.

42. C

Free verse poetry contains neither rhyme nor meter.

43. B

Emergent literacy refers to the language development that occurs before a child can read or write words. These skills are developed from birth and include listening, speaking, memory, recognizing pattern and rhyme, print awareness, critical thinking, and the development of the fine motor skills necessary for writing.

44. B

An idiom is a phrase that has come to have a different meaning through usage than the meanings of its individual words. Different languages have very different idioms and because it is difficult to ascertain the meaning of an idiom from the words it contains (without the prior cultural background knowledge), idioms can be particularly tricky for second language learners.

45. B

Phoneme substitution is an exercise in which one phoneme of a word is replaced with another phoneme to create a new word.

46. D

The indirect object is the one that is receiving the action of the verb. In this case, the book is being loaned TO Lauren, making her the indirect object.

47. D

All of these share the common root "script" which means "write."

48. C

Fascist regimes came to power in Europe after World War I and their rise was a cause of World War II.

49. D

Senators have the longest single term length, at six years. Presidents and vice-presidents serve four-year terms, while members of the House of Representatives serve for two year terms.

50. C

Vermont was not one of the Thirteen Colonies.

51. C

The Thirteenth Amendment abolished slavery and was adopted soon after the Civil War.

52. C

Big business was fairly unregulated in the 19th century, which led to much abuse. Regulations to protect consumers were put into place in the 20th century.

53. B

The caste system was the rigid traditional social class system in India, closely tied to Hinduism.

54. D

Republics and parliamentary systems provide the people with representatives and a democracy allows citizens to vote. People have very little say in an autocracy, in which the government is run by a single authoritarian ruler.

55. B

Terrace farming is an adaptation that humans have made to allow them to farm on mountainsides.

56. C

The balance of trade refers to the ratio of exports to imports that a country has over a period of time. A favorable balance of trade is one in which a country exports more than it imports.

57. C

All of these were explorers from Europe.

58. D

All of these should be considered when evaluating historical texts.

59. A

The Mississippi Delta is located in Louisiana and connects the river to the Gulf of Mexico.

1. B
The product rule of exponents states: $a^n \cdot a^m = a^{n+m}$

2. B
$21/25 * 100 = 84$

3. A
You can solve this problem by drawing a tree diagram of the possibilities, by listing out the possible combinations, or by using multiplication. 2 choices for sandwiches multiplied by 3 choices for drinks equals 6 possible combinations.

4. A
It is important to follow the order of operations (PEMDAS).

5. A
The factors of 15 are 1, 3, 5, and 15. The factors of 18 are 1, 2, 3, 6, 9, and 18. The greatest common factor is 3.

6. A
Absolute value is a number's distance from zero and is always a positive number.

7. B
The two numbers are 6 and 2. $6 * 2 = 12$ and $6 - 2 = 4$.

8. D
The additive inverse of a number is its equal opposite such that the two numbers added together would equal zero. $4 + (-4) = 0$

9. A
If 25 shirts cost $50 from the manufacturer, the cost per shirt is $2. For 80 shirts, the cost would be $160. The sale price per shirt is $8, which comes to $640 for 80 shirts. Profit = price - cost. $640 - $160 = $480

10. C
The first step in the order of operations is to take care of operations within parentheses.

11. B

When comparing decimals, move from left to right. A, B, and C all have a 3 in the tenths place. In the hundredths place, choice B has a 1, which is the smallest of the given values.

12. C

Lines that never touch are parallel. Perpendicular lines intersect at a right angle. The terms complimentary and supplementary refer to angles, not lines.

13. C

Any number raised to the 0 power equals 1.

14. B

Solve by setting up a proportion.

15. A

The slope formula is $m = \frac{y_2 - y_1}{x_2 - x_1}$.

16. A

The formula for the area of a triangle is A =1/2 bh. In this case, the triangle is right so the two shorter sides will represent the base and the height. (The longest side in a right triangle is always the hypotenuse.) 1/2 * 3 * 4 = 6

17. C

This is a set of perfect squares.

18. A

The commutative property states that in a multiplication or addition problem, the order of the numbers being added or multiplied does not affect the final result.

19. A

The only one of these choices that is a multiple of 4 and 5 is 20.

20. C

72% of 25 is 18 (25 * 0.75 = 18). That means there are 18 males in the class. To find out how many females there are, subtract the number of males from the total.

21. B

To find the median, put the scores in numerical order. The median is the number is the middle. In order, the numbers read: 76, 80, 88, 92, 94. The number in the middle is 88.

22. B

To find the mean, add up the scores and divide by the number of scores (5).

23. A

Remember to switch the inequality sign when dividing each side by a negative number.

24. B

Angles that measure between 90° and 180° are considered obtuse.

25. A

9 students like summer the best and 2 students like fall the best. $9 - 2 = 7$

26. B

A prime number can only be divided evenly by itself and 1. 2 is the only even number that is prime because every other even number can be divided by 2.

27. C

All sides and angles of a triangle are equal therefore each angle in an equilateral triangle must equal 60°.

28. C

The Pythagorean Theorem is $a^2 + b^2 = c^2$, where a and b are the lengths of the legs of a right triangle and c is the length of the hypotenuse.

29. B

32 is a multiple of 16, not a factor.

30. B

$7/8 = 0.875$

31. A

Dividing by zero always yields a result that is undefined.

32. C

2/6 is equal to 1/3. All of the other choices are equal to 1/2.

33. A

A trapezoid has one set of parallel sides. All of the other figures listed have two pairs of parallel sides, which classifies them as parallelograms.

34. D

The even numbers in this set are 2, 4, and 6. That means that there are 3 favorable outcomes out of 6 possible outcomes. The probability of getting an even number is 3/6, which reduces to 1/2.

35. B

To get from one member of the set to the next, multiply by 4. A set whose rule is solely multiplication is called a geometric set.

36. C

98 has factors other than itself and 1, so it is not prime.

37. D

Convert 2 hours and 30 minutes to 2.5 hours. 55 miles per hour multiplied by 2.5 hours equals 137.5 miles.

38. C

Multiples are the result of multiplying a number by positive integers. 6 * 1 = 6; 6 * 2 = 12;   6 * 3 = 18; etc.

39. D

The crust is the surface of the Earth on which life exists.

40. A

The food chain shows how energy gets from producers (plants) that make energy to consumers (animals) that get the energy through eating plants and other animals.

41. A

In a lunar eclipse, the Earth is directly between the sun and the Moon, blocking light from hitting the Moon.

42. D

A compound is the result of chemical bonding of two or more elements.

43. D

Metal is the best conductor. The other materials are considered insulators because electricity cannot easily pass through them.

44. A

The faster the vibrations, the higher the pitch.

45. D

While peer review can be helpful, it is not an essential step in the Scientific Method.

46. B

Information about the elements can be found on the periodic table.

47. C

The tilt of the Earth on its axis determines how direct the solar radiation a location receives will be.

48. C

Mercury is the closest planet to the sun.

49. A

Natural selection is the process by which those traits that are beneficial to organisms are produced and passed on in the species. Natural selection is based on a premise of the "survival of the fittest," which says that those organisms best genetically equipped to survive and reproduce will and will have their traits passed on. Those organisms that are weaker will eventually die off and with them, their less favorable traits.

50. A

"Meteorite" is the name given to meteoroids once they enter Earth's atmosphere.

51. C

The idea that an object in motion will stay in motion and an object at rest will stay at rest unless acted upon by an outside force is known as inertia. This is part of Newton's First Law of Motion.

52. B

The water cycle is responsible for precipitation, which is a major component of weather.

53. C

The nucleus of an animal (or plant) cell contains the organism's DNA.

54. B

The nucleus of an atom contains protons, which have a positive charge, and neutrons, which have a neutral charge, making the overall charge of the nucleus positive.

55. D

A wheel and axle is the most helpful simple machine for moving an object across a horizontal distance. Pulleys and levers are more useful for vertical distances, while wedges are used for cutting or splitting.

56. D

Some organisms use sexual reproduction, while others utilize asexual reproduction.

57. B

Condensation occurs when a gas cools enough to change into a liquid.

58. B

Humans are classified as animalia (animals).

59. A

Magnets have two poles- North and South. Like poles repel and opposite poles attract.

60. C

In surface run-off, water remains in liquid form. Run-off occurs when the soil becomes oversaturated with water and the excess comes to the surface and flows over land.

61. C

Convergent plates are plates that collide, which can result in the creation of volcanoes.

62. B

Only plant cells contain chloroplasts, which are the site of photosynthesis.

63. D

For a recessive trait to be displayed, the offspring must have two genes for the recessive trait. If both parents have only recessive genes, the offspring will also have the recessive genes.

64. A

Gases are the least dense. The particles move rapidly and spread to take the volume of their container.

65. C

Tension force is the force present in a wire, cable, or cord when forces pull on both ends.

66. A

Fission is the splitting of atoms. Fission is the type of reaction used to create atomic bombs and nuclear reactors.

67. D

All of these help to prevent the spread of disease.

68. A

Value is the lightness or darkness of a shape. Shades are darker in value and tints are lighter.

69. C

The circulatory system transports blood throughout the human body through veins and arteries.

70. C

Standing on one foot helps develop balance, which is a non-locomotor skill.

71. C

Force is the energy used to create motion in dance. Space is the area in which the dance takes place. Direction (which way the movement is going), level (how high off the ground the movement is occurring), and pathway (the path the movement takes) are all elements of space.

72. B

Slowed responses are a common effect of depressants.

73. D

In drama, comedies are plays that result in a happy ending for the main character. They are usually light-hearted, but not always funny. Comedies are the opposite of tragedies, wherein the main character has an unhappy ending, often as a consequences of his own choices.

74. C

Tempo is the speed of a piece of music and is related to rhythm.

75. B

Locomotor skills involve travelling movement from place to place. Throwing is considered a manipulative skill because it involves the use of equipment.

CPSIA information can be obtained at www.ICGtesting.com
Printed in the USA
LVOW02s0307131014

408473LV00007B/68/P